2ND EDITION

Ventures 3

STUDENT'S BOOK

Gretchen Bitterlin   Dennis Johnson   Donna Price   Sylvia Ramirez

K. Lynn Savage (Series Editor)

CAMBRIDGE
UNIVERSITY PRESS

CAMBRIDGE
UNIVERSITY PRESS

University Printing House, Cambridge CB2 8BS, United Kingdom

One Liberty Plaza, 20th Floor, New York, NY 10006, USA

477 Williamstown Road, Port Melbourne, VIC 3207, Australia

4843/24, 2nd Floor, Ansari Road, Daryaganj, Delhi – 110002, India

79 Anson Road, #06–04/06, Singapore 079906

Cambridge University Press is part of the University of Cambridge.

It furthers the University's mission by disseminating knowledge in the pursuit of education, learning and research at the highest international levels of excellence.

www.cambridge.org
Information on this title: www.cambridge.org/9781107684720

First published 2008
20 19 18 17 16 15 14 13 12 11 10 9

Printed in Mexico by Editorial Impresora Apolo, S.A. de C.V.

A catalogue record for this publication is available from the British Library

ISBN 978-1-107-68472-0 Student's Book with Audio CD
ISBN 978-1-107-64001-6 Workbook with Audio CD
ISBN 978-1-139-88472-3 Online Workbook
ISBN 978-1-107-65217-0 Teacher's Edition with Assessment Audio CD / CD-ROM
ISBN 978-1-107-66076-2 Class Audio CDs
ISBN 978-1-107-64952-1 Presentation Plus

Additional resources for this publication at www.cambridge.org/ventures

Art direction, book design, photo research, and layout services: Q2A / Bill Smith
Audio production: CityVox, LLC

Authors' acknowledgments

The authors would like to acknowledge and thank focus group participants and reviewers for their insightful comments, as well as Cambridge University Press editorial, marketing, and production staffs, whose thorough research and attention to detail have resulted in a quality product.

The publishers would also like to extend their particular thanks to the following reviewers and consultants for their valuable insights and suggestions:

Kit Bell, LAUSD division of Adult and Career Education, Los Angeles, CA; **Bethany Bogage**, San Diego Community College District, San Diego, CA; **Leslie Keaton Boyd**, Dallas ISD, Dallas, TX; **Barbara Brodsky**, Teaching Work Readiness English for Refugees – Lutheran Family Services, Omaha, NE; **Jessica Buchsbaum**, City College of San Francisco, San Francisco, CA; **Helen Butner**, University of the Fraser Valley, British Columbia, Canada; **Sharon Churchill Roe**, Acadia University, Wolfville, NS, Canada; **Lisa Dolehide**, San Mateo Adult School, San Mateo, CA; **Yadira M. Dominguez**, Dallas ISD, Dallas, TX; **Donna M. Douglas**, College of DuPage, Glen Ellyn, IL; **Latarsha Dykes**, Broward Collge, Pembroke Pines, FL; **Megan L. Ernst**, Glendale Community College, Glendale, CA; **Megan Esler**, Portland Community College, Portland, OR; **Jennifer Fadden**, Fairfax County Public Schools, Fairfax, VA; **Fotine Fahouris**, College of Marin, Kentfield, CA; **Lynn Francis, M.A, M.S.**, San Diego Community College, San Diego, CA; **Danielle Gines**, Tarrant County College, Arlington, TX; **Katherine Hayne**, College of Marin, Kentfield, CA; **Armenuhi Hovhannes**, City College of San Francisco, San Francisco, CA; **Fayne B. Johnson**; **Martha L. Koranda**, College of DuPage, Glen Ellyn, IL; **Daphne Lagios**, San Mateo Adult School, San Mateo, CA, **Judy Langelier**, School District of Palm Beach County, Wellington, FL; **Janet Les**, Chilliwack Community Services, Chilliwack, British Columbia, Canada; **Keila Louzada**, Northern Virginia Community College, Sterling, VA; **Karen Mauer**, Fort Worth ISD, Fort Worth, TX; **Silvana Mehner**, Northern Virginia Community College, Sterling, VA; **Astrid T. Mendez-Gines,** Tarrant County College, Arlington, TX; **Beverly A. Miller**, Houston Community College, Houston, TX; **José Montes, MS. Ed.**, The English Center, Miami-Dade County Public Schools, Miami, FL; **Suzi Monti**, Community College of Baltimore County, Baltimore, MD; **Irina Morgunova**, Roxbury Community College, Roxbury Crossing, MA; **Julia Morgunova**, Roxbury Community College, Roxbury Crossing, MA; **Susan Otero**, Fairfax County Public Schools, Fairfax, VA; **Sergei Paromchik**, Hillsborough County Public Schools, Tampa, FL; **Pearl W. Pigott**, Houston Community College, Houston, TX; **Marlene Ramirez**, The English Center, Miami-Dade County Public Schools, Miami, FL; **Cory Rayala**, Harbor Service Center, LAUSD, Los Angeles, CA; **Catherine M. Rifkin**, Florida State College at Jacksonville, Jacksonville, FL; **Danette Roe**, Evans Community Adult School, Los Angeles, CA; **Maria Roy**, Kilgore College, Kilgore, TX; **Jill Shalongo**, Glendale Community College, Glendale, CA, and Sierra Linda High School, Phoenix, AZ; **Laurel Owensby Slater**, San Diego Community College District, San Diego, CA; **Rheba Smith**, San Diego Community College District, San Diego, CA; **Jennifer Snyder**, Portland Community College, Portland, OR; **Mary K. Solberg**, Metropolitan Community College, Omaha, NE; **Rosanne Vitola**, Austin Community College, Austin, TX

Scope and sequence

UNIT TITLE TOPIC	FUNCTIONS	LISTENING AND SPEAKING	VOCABULARY	GRAMMAR FOCUS
Welcome pages 2–5	▪ Discussing goals ▪ Filling out a goal form ▪ Discussing past and future events	▪ Listening and asking about goals ▪ Asking about daily routines ▪ Listening about events in the past and future	▪ Review of time phrases	Verb tense review: ▪ present and present continuous ▪ past and future
Unit 1 **Personal information** pages 6–17 Topic: **Personality traits**	▪ Describing and comparing likes and interests ▪ Describing and discussing personality types	▪ Asking about and comparing preferences ▪ Describing personality types	▪ Personal interests ▪ Personality types ▪ Adjectives that describe people	▪ Verbs + gerunds ▪ Comparisons with *more than*, *less than*, *as much as* ▪ *must* for logical conclusions
Unit 2 **At school** pages 18–29 Topic: **Study skills**	▪ Discussing study problems and learning strategies ▪ Offering advice ▪ Inquiring about people's experiences	▪ Asking about study problems and learning strategies ▪ Asking about someone's recent past	▪ Study problems ▪ Learning strategies	▪ Present perfect with *how long*, *for*, *since* ▪ Present perfect questions with *ever*; short answers ▪ Simple past and present perfect
Review: Units 1 and 2 pages 30–31		▪ Understanding a conversation		
Unit 3 **Friends and family** pages 32–43 Topic: **Neighbors**	▪ Offering help ▪ Agreeing and disagreeing ▪ Giving reasons ▪ Making a complaint	▪ Asking about and describing problems ▪ Giving reasons ▪ Discussing borrowing and lending	▪ *borrow* vs. *lend* ▪ Two-word verbs	▪ *because of* phrases and *because* clauses ▪ *too* and *enough* ▪ *be able to*
Unit 4 **Health** pages 44–55 Topic: **Healthy habits**	▪ Discussing healthy foods and exercise ▪ Describing events in the recent past ▪ Describing past habits	▪ Asking about staying healthy ▪ Asking about past and present health habits	▪ Healthy habits and routines ▪ Beneficial plants	▪ Present perfect with *recently* and *lately* ▪ *used to* ▪ Reported commands
Review: Units 3 and 4 pages 56–57		▪ Understanding a conversation		
Unit 5 **Around town** pages 58–69 Topic: **Community resources and events**	▪ Discussing future plans ▪ Describing actions based on expectations ▪ Describing community events	▪ Asking about people's plans ▪ Asking about people's expectations ▪ Talking about community events	▪ Entertainment ▪ Positive and negative adjectives	▪ Verbs + infinitives ▪ Present perfect with *already* and *yet* ▪ Verbs + infinitives and verbs + gerunds

READING	WRITING	LIFE SKILLS	PRONUNCIATION
▪ Reading a paragraph about goals	▪ Writing your goal and steps to reach it	▪ Talking about your goal and steps to reach it	▪ Pronouncing key vocabulary
▪ Reading an article about personality and jobs ▪ Predicting content from titles and pictures	▪ Writing a descriptive paragraph with a topic sentence and supporting sentences ▪ Using adjectives	▪ Understanding a bar graph ▪ Scanning a Web page for information	▪ Pronouncing key vocabulary
▪ Reading an article about strategies for learning English ▪ Using context to identify parts of speech ▪ Locating examples that support statements	▪ Writing a paragraph with examples to support ideas ▪ Using examples to support your ideas	▪ Reading and understanding tips for taking tests ▪ Talking about strategies for learning English	▪ Pronouncing key vocabulary
			▪ Stressing content words
▪ Reading a newsletter about a neighborhood watch ▪ Identifying the main idea, facts, and examples	▪ Writing a letter of complaint ▪ Supporting the main idea with examples	▪ Reading and understanding an ad for volunteers ▪ Writing a letter of complaint	▪ Pronouncing key vocabulary
▪ Reading an article about beneficial plants ▪ Identifying the topic from the introduction and conclusion ▪ Identifying parts of word families	▪ Writing a descriptive paragraph ▪ Writing a topic sentence ▪ Completing a chart	▪ Completing a medical history form ▪ Talking about how to stay healthy	▪ Pronouncing key vocabulary
			▪ Voiced and voiceless *th* sounds
▪ Reading a review of a concert ▪ Using context to distinguish between positive and negative words	▪ Writing an e-mail ▪ Completing a graphic organizer	▪ Reading and understanding announcements about community events ▪ Talking about community events	▪ Pronouncing key vocabulary

UNIT TITLE TOPIC	FUNCTIONS	LISTENING AND SPEAKING	VOCABULARY	GRAMMAR FOCUS
Unit 6 **Time** pages 70–81 Topic: **Time management**	▪ Prioritizing ▪ Discussing how to manage time ▪ Giving advice ▪ Describing habits	▪ Prioritizing tasks ▪ Asking about habits and daily activities ▪ Contrasting qualities and habits of good and weak time managers	▪ Time-management ▪ Prefixes meaning *not* ▪ Idioms with time	▪ Adverb clauses with *when* ▪ Adverb clauses with *before* and *after* ▪ *one / some / any* and *it / them*
Review: Units 5 and 6 pages 82–83		▪ Understanding a conversation		
Unit 7 **Shopping** pages 84–95 Topic: **Saving and spending**	▪ Making suggestions ▪ Asking for and giving advice ▪ Discussing financial concerns ▪ Comparing banking services	▪ Asking and answering questions about buying on credit ▪ Making suggestions and giving advice	▪ Banking and finances ▪ Compound nouns	▪ *could* and *should* ▪ Gerunds after prepositions ▪ Collocations with *get* and *take*
Unit 8 **Work** pages 96–107 Topic: **Finding a job**	▪ Discussing work-related goals ▪ Discussing ways to find a job ▪ Identifying procedures involved with a job interview	▪ Talking about a job interview ▪ Asking about ongoing activities	▪ Employment ▪ Separable phrasal verbs	▪ Present perfect continuous ▪ Separable phrasal verbs ▪ Present continuous and present perfect continuous
Review: Units 7 and 8 pages 108–109		▪ Understanding a conversation		
Unit 9 **Daily living** pages 110–121 Topic: **Community action**	▪ Describing past activities ▪ Describing past events	▪ Describing a crime ▪ Describing past actions ▪ Asking about an emergency ▪ Discussing safety items	▪ Crimes ▪ Emergency situations ▪ Time phrases	▪ Past continuous ▪ Past continuous and simple past with *when* and *while* ▪ Three uses of the present continuous
Unit 10 **Free time** pages 122–133 Topic: **Vacation plans**	▪ Describing future possibility ▪ Describing a sequence of events in the future	▪ Describing vacation plans ▪ Asking about future possibility ▪ Describing the sequence of future events	▪ Travel and vacation	▪ Future real conditionals ▪ Future time clauses with *before* and *after* ▪ Three uses of the present perfect
Review: Units 9 and 10 pages 134–135		▪ Understanding a news report		

READING	WRITING	LIFE SKILLS	PRONUNCIATION
▪ Reading an article about cultural time rules ▪ Recognizing dashes that introduce examples ▪ Identifying words with prefixes meaning *not*	▪ Writing a descriptive paragraph about a good or weak time manager ▪ Using a signal before the conclusion	▪ Reading and understanding a pie chart ▪ Talking about how to manage time	▪ Pronouncing key vocabulary
			▪ Initial *st* sound
▪ Reading an article about credit card debt ▪ Identifying problems and solutions discussed in a text	▪ Giving advice about saving money ▪ Using *first*, *second*, *third*, and *finally* to organize ideas	▪ Reading and understanding a brochure comparing checking accounts ▪ Talking about credit, credit cards, and debt	▪ Pronouncing key vocabulary
▪ Reading a blog about a job search ▪ Scanning for specific information ▪ Using a dictionary to select the best definition for a context	▪ Writing a formal thank-you letter ▪ Understanding what to include in a thank-you letter	▪ Reading and understanding a chart comparing job growth ▪ Preparing for a job interview ▪ Reading and understanding a blog	▪ Pronouncing key vocabulary
			▪ Linking sounds
▪ Reading an article about an emergency ▪ Recognizing time phrases ▪ Guessing meaning from context	▪ Writing about an emergency ▪ Using *Who*, *What*, *When*, *Where*, *Why*, and *How*	▪ Reading and understanding a chart comparing safety in various U.S. states ▪ Talking about emergency situations	▪ Pronouncing key vocabulary
▪ Reading an article about Alcatraz ▪ Using clues to guess the meaning of words	▪ Writing about a tourist attraction ▪ Using complex sentences to add variety	▪ Reading and understanding hotel brochures ▪ Talking about travel arrangements	▪ Pronouncing key vocabulary
			▪ Unstressed vowel sound

To the teacher

What is *Ventures*?

Ventures is a six-level, four-skills, standards-based, integrated-skills series that empowers students to achieve their academic and career goals.

■ This most complete program with a wealth of resources provides instructors with the tools for any teaching situation.

■ The new Online Workbook keeps students learning outside the classroom.

■ Easy-to-teach materials make for a more productive classroom.

What components does *Ventures* have?

Student's Book with Audio CD

Each of the core **Student's Books** contains ten topic-focused units, interspersed with five review units. The main units feature six skill-focused lessons.

■ **Lessons** in the Student's Book are self-contained, allowing for completion within a one-hour class period.

■ **Review lessons** recycle and reinforce the listening, vocabulary, and grammar skills developed in the two prior units and include a pronunciation activity.

■ **Self-assessments** in the back of the book give students an opportunity to reflect on their learning. They support learner persistence and help determine whether students are ready for the unit test.

■ **Reference charts**, also in the back of the book, provide grammar paradigms and rules for spelling, punctuation, and grammar.

■ References to the **Self-study audio CD** that accompanies the Student's Book are indicated in the Student's Book by an icon and track number: Look for the audio icon and track number to find activities with self-study audio. "STUDENT" refers to the self-study audio, and "CLASS" refers to the class audio. A full class audio is available separately.

STUDENT TK 10
CLASS CD1 TK 14

■ A **Student Arcade**, available online at www.cambridge.org/venturesarcade, allows students to practice their skills with interactive activities and download self-study audio.

Teacher's Edition with Assessment Audio CD / CD-ROM

The interleaved **Teacher's Edition** includes easy-to-follow lesson plans for every unit.

■ Tips and suggestions address common areas of difficulty for students and provide suggestions for expansion activities and improving learner persistence.

■ A **More Ventures** chart at the end of each lesson indicates where to find additional practice material in other *Ventures* components such as the Workbook, Online Teacher's Resource Room (see below), and Student Arcade.

■ Unit, midterm, and final tests, which include listening, vocabulary, grammar, reading, and writing sections, are found in the back of the Teacher's Edition.

■ The **Assessment Audio CD / CD-ROM** that accompanies the Teacher's Edition contains the audio for each unit, midterm, and final test. It also features all the tests in customizable format so teachers can customize them to suit their needs.

Online Teacher's Resource Room (www.cambridge.org/myresourceroom)

Ventures 2nd Edition offers a free Online Teacher's Resource Room where teachers can download hundreds of additional worksheets and classroom materials including:

■ A *placement test* that helps place students into appropriate levels of *Ventures*.

■ A *Career and Educational Pathways* solution that helps students identify their educational and career goals.

■ *Collaborative activities* for each lesson in Levels 1–4 that develop cooperative learning and community building within the classroom.

■ *Writing worksheets* that help Literacy-level students recognize and write shapes, letters, and numbers, while alphabet and number cards promote partner and group work.

■ *Picture dictionary cards and worksheets* that reinforce vocabulary learned in Levels Basic, 1, and 2.

■ *Extended readings and worksheets* that provide added reading skills development for Levels 3 and 4.

■ *Add Ventures* worksheets that were designed for use in multilevel classrooms and in leveled classes where the proficiency level of students differs.

Log on to www.cambridge.org/myresourceroom to explore these and hundreds of other free resources.

Workbook with Audio CD

The **Workbook** provides two pages of activities for each lesson in the Student's Book and includes an audio CD.

- If used in class, the Workbook can extend classroom instructional time by 30 minutes per lesson.
- The exercises are designed so learners can complete them in class or independently. Students can check their answers with the answer key in the back of the Workbook. Workbook exercises can be assigned in class, for homework, or as student support when a class is missed.
- Grammar charts at the back of the Workbook allow students to use the Workbook for self-study.

Online Workbooks

The self-grading **Online Workbooks** offer programs the flexibility of introducing blended learning.

- They provide the same high-quality practice opportunities as the print Workbooks and give students instant feedback.
- They allow teachers and programs to track student progress and time on task.

Unit organization

Each unit has six skill-focused lessons:

LESSON A Listening focuses students on the unit topic. The initial exercise, ***Before you listen***, creates student interest with visuals that help the teacher assess what learners already know and serve as a prompt for the unit's key vocabulary. Next is ***Listen***, which is based on conversations. Students relate vocabulary to meaning and relate the spoken and written forms of new theme-related vocabulary. ***After you listen*** concludes the lesson by practicing language related to the theme in a communicative activity, either orally with a partner or individually in a writing activity.

LESSONS B AND C focus on grammar. The lessons move from a ***Grammar focus*** that presents the grammar point in chart form; to ***Practice*** exercises that check comprehension of the grammar point and provide guided practice; and, finally, to ***Communicate*** exercises that guide learners as they generate original

answers and conversations. These lessons often include a *Culture note*, which provides information directly related to the conversation practice (such as the use of titles with last names), or a *Useful language* note, which introduces useful expressions and functional language.

LESSON D Reading develops reading skills and expands vocabulary. The lesson opens with a ***Before you read*** exercise, designed to activate prior knowledge and encourage learners to make predictions. A *Reading tip*, which focuses on a specific reading skill, accompanies the ***Read*** exercise. The reading section of the lesson concludes with ***After you read*** exercises that check comprehension. In Levels Basic, 1, and 2, the vocabulary expansion portion of the lesson is a ***Picture dictionary***. It includes a *word bank*, pictures to identify, and a conversation for practicing the new words. The words expand vocabulary related to the unit topic. In Books 3 and 4, the vocabulary expansion portion of the lesson uses new vocabulary from the reading to build skills such as recognizing word families, selecting definitions based on the context of the reading, and using clues in the reading to guess meaning.

LESSON E Writing provides practice with process writing within the context of the unit. ***Before you write*** exercises provide warm-up activities to activate the language needed for the writing assignment, followed by one or more exercises that provide a model for students to follow when they write. A *Writing tip* presents information about punctuation or paragraph organization directly related to the writing assignment. The ***Write*** exercise sets goals for the student writing. In the ***After you write*** exercise, students share with a partner.

LESSON F Another view has three sections. ***Life-skills reading*** develops the scanning and skimming skills used with documents such as forms, charts, schedules, announcements, and ads. Multiple-choice questions (modeled on CASAS[1] and BEST[2]) develop test-taking skills. ***Grammar connections***, in Levels 1–4, contrasts grammar points and includes guided practice and communicative activities. Finally, ***Wrap up*** refers students to the self-assessment page in the back of the book, where they can check their knowledge and evaluate their progress.

---

[1] The Comprehensive Adult Student Assessment System. For more information, see www.casas.org.

[2] The Basic English Skills Test. For more information, see www.cal.org/BEST.

Unit tour

The Most Complete Course for Student Success

Ventures empowers students to achieve their academic and career goals.

■ The most complete program with a wealth of resources provides instructors with the tools for any teaching situation.

■ The new Online Workbook keeps students learning outside the classroom.

■ Easy-to-teach materials make for a more productive classroom.

The Big Picture

• Introduces the unit topic and provides rich opportunities for classroom discussion.

• Activates students' prior knowledge and previews the unit vocabulary.

Unit Goals

• Explicit unit goals ensure student involvement in the learning process.

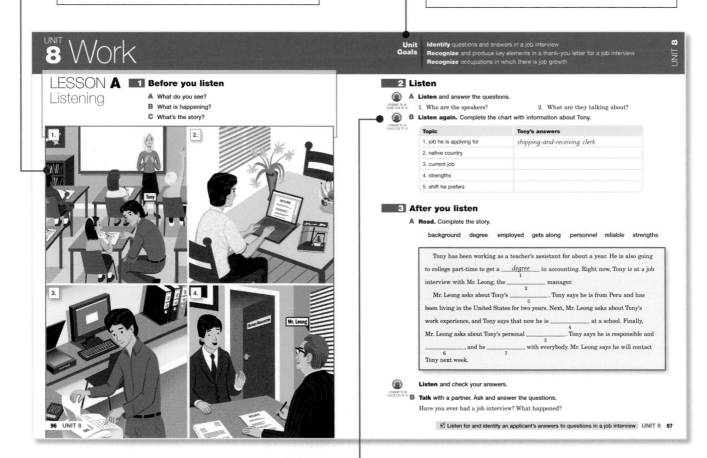

Two Different Audio Programs

• Class audio features over 100 minutes of listening practice and improves listening comprehension.

• Self-study audio encourages learner persistence and autonomy.

• Easy navigation between the two with clear track listings.

Grammar Chart

- Clear grammar charts with additional grammar reference in the back of the book allow for greater teacher flexibility.

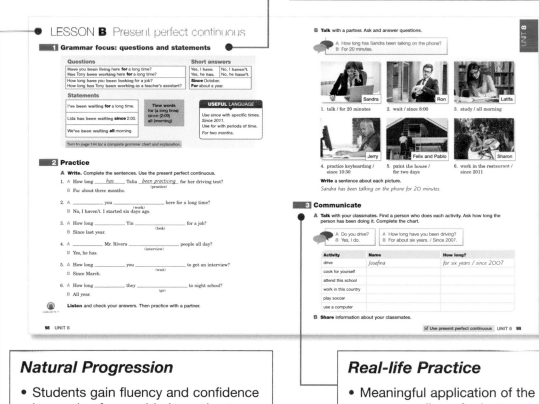

Natural Progression

- Students gain fluency and confidence by moving from guided practice to communicative activities.

Real-life Practice

- Meaningful application of the grammar allows for better student engagement.

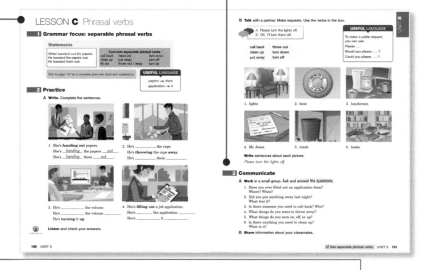

Every unit has two grammar lessons that follow the same structure.

Reading

- *Ventures* features a three-step reading approach that highlights reading strategies and skills needed for success: **Before you read, Read, After you read.**

Building Vocabulary

- Explicit dictionary skills instruction expands students' vocabulary.

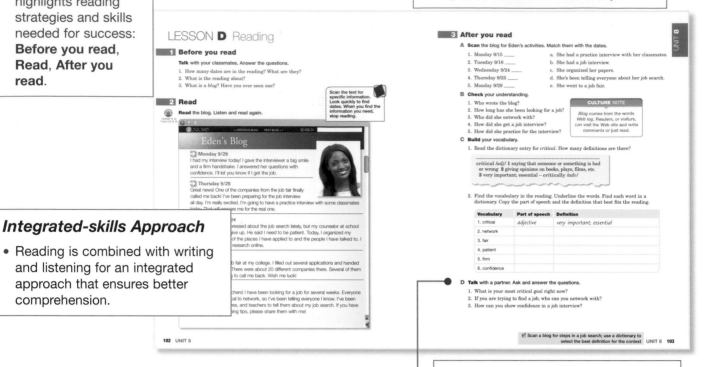

LESSON D Reading

1 Before you read

Talk with your classmates. Answer the questions.
1. How many dates are in the reading? What are they?
2. What is the reading about?
3. What is a *blog*? Have you ever seen one?

2 Read

Read the blog. Listen and read again.

> Scan the text for specific information. Look quickly to find dates. When you find the information you need, stop reading.

Eden's Blog

Monday 9/29
I had my interview today! I gave the interviewer a big smile and a firm handshake. I answered her questions with confidence. I'll let you know if I get the job.

Thursday 9/25
Great news! One of the companies from the job fair finally called me back! I've been preparing for the job interview all day. I'm really excited. I'm going to have a practice interview with some classmates today. That will prepare me for the real one.

...ressed about the job search lately, but my counselor at school ...ive up. He said I need to be patient. Today, I organized my ...of the places I have applied to and the people I have talked to. I... ...research online.

...b fair at my college. I filled out several applications and handed ...There were about 20 different companies there. Several of them ...g to call me back. Wish me luck!

...chers! I have been looking for a job for several weeks. Everyone ...cal to network, so I've been telling everyone I know. I've been ...es, and teachers to tell them about my job search. If you have ...ing tips, please share them with me!

102 UNIT 8

3 After you read

A Scan the blog for Eden's activities. Match them with the dates.

1. Monday 9/15 ____   a. She had a practice interview with her classmates.
2. Tuesday 9/16 ____   b. She had a job interview.
3. Wednesday 9/24 ____   c. She organized her papers.
4. Thursday 9/25 ____   d. She's been telling everyone about her job search.
5. Monday 9/29 ____   e. She went to a job fair.

B Check your understanding.
1. Who wrote the blog?
2. How long has she been looking for a job?
3. Who did she network with?
4. How did she get a job interview?
5. How did she practice for the interview?

CULTURE NOTE
Blog comes from the words *Web log*. Readers, or visitors, can visit the Web site and write comments or just read.

C Build your vocabulary.
1. Read the dictionary entry for *critical*. How many definitions are there?

> **critical** /adj/ **1** saying that someone or something is bad or wrong **2** giving opinions on books, plays, films, etc. **3** very important; essential – **critically** /adv/

2. Find the vocabulary in the reading. Underline the words. Find each word in a dictionary. Copy the part of speech and the definition that best fits the reading.

Vocabulary	Part of speech	Definition
1. critical	adjective	very important; essential
2. network		
3. fair		
4. patient		
5. firm		
6. confidence		

D Talk with a partner. Ask and answer the questions.
1. What is your most critical goal right now?
2. If you are trying to find a job, who can you network with?
3. How can you show confidence in a job interview?

☑ Scan a blog for steps in a job search; use a dictionary to select the best definition for the context UNIT 8 103

Integrated-skills Approach

- Reading is combined with writing and listening for an integrated approach that ensures better comprehension.

Talk with a Partner

- Spoken practice helps students internalize the vocabulary and relate it to their lives.

Process Writing

- *Ventures* includes a robust process-writing approach: prewriting, writing, and peer review.

Writing for Success

- *Ventures* writing lessons are academic and purposeful, which moves students toward work and educational goals.

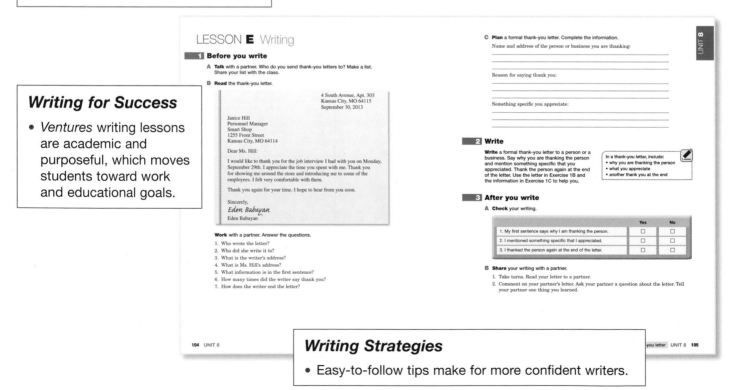

LESSON E Writing

1 Before you write

A Talk with a partner. Who do you send thank-you letters to? Make a list. Share your list with the class.

B Read the thank-you letter.

> 4 South Avenue, Apt. 303
> Kansas City, MO 64115
> September 30, 2013
>
> Janice Hill
> Personnel Manager
> Smart Shop
> 1255 Front Street
> Kansas City, MO 64114
>
> Dear Ms. Hill:
>
> I would like to thank you for the job interview I had with you on Monday, September 29th. I appreciate the time you spent with me. Thank you for showing me around the store and introducing me to some of the employees. I felt very comfortable with them.
>
> Thank you again for your time. I hope to hear from you soon.
>
> Sincerely,
> *Eden Babayan*
> Eden Babayan

Work with a partner. Answer the questions.
1. Who wrote the letter?
2. Who did she write it to?
3. What is the writer's address?
4. What is Ms. Hill's address?
5. What information is in the first sentence?
6. How many times did the writer say thank you?
7. How does the writer end the letter?

C Plan a formal thank-you letter. Complete the information.

Name and address of the person or business you are thanking:

Reason for saying thank you:

Something specific you appreciate:

2 Write

Write a formal thank-you letter to a person or a business. Say why you are thanking the person and mention something specific that you appreciated. Thank the person again at the end of the letter. Use the letter in Exercise 1B and the information in Exercise 1C to help you.

> In a thank-you letter, include:
> • why you are thanking the person
> • what you appreciate
> • another thank you at the end

3 After you write

A Check your writing.

	Yes	No
1. My first sentence says why I am thanking the person.	☐	☐
2. I mentioned something specific that I appreciated.	☐	☐
3. I thanked the person again at the end of the letter.	☐	☐

B Share your writing with a partner.
1. Take turns. Read your letter to a partner.
2. Comment on your partner's letter. Ask your partner a question about the letter. Tell your partner one thing you learned.

104 UNIT 8

...you letter UNIT 8 105

Writing Strategies

- Easy-to-follow tips make for more confident writers.

Document Literacy

- Explicit practice with authentic-type documents builds real-life skills.

Grammar Connections

- Contrasting two grammar forms in a communicative way helps with grammar accuracy.

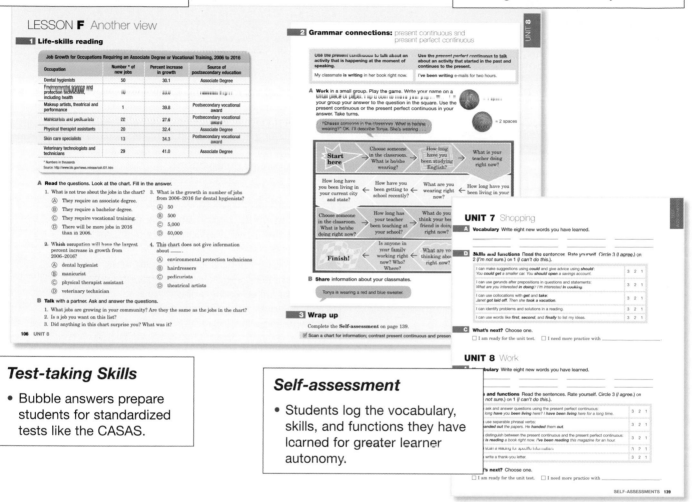

Test-taking Skills

- Bubble answers prepare students for standardized tests like the CASAS.

Self-assessment

- Students log the vocabulary, skills, and functions they have learned for greater learner autonomy.

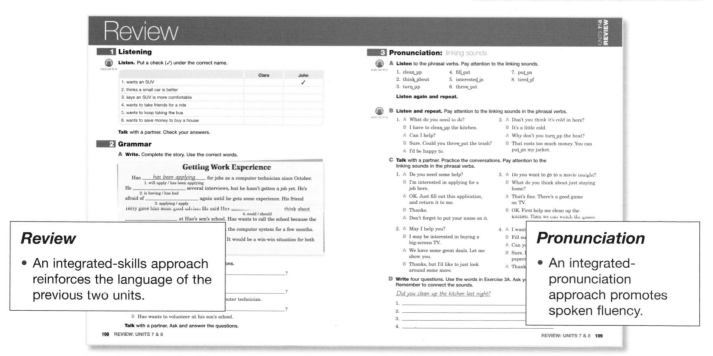

Review

- An integrated-skills approach reinforces the language of the previous two units.

Pronunciation

- An integrated-pronunciation approach promotes spoken fluency.

Correlations

UNIT	CASAS Competencies	NRS Educational Functioning Level Descriptors *Oral BEST: 42–50 (SPL 4)* *BEST Plus: 439–472 (SPL 4)* *BEST Literacy: 47–53 (SPL 4)*
Unit 1 **Personal information** Pages 6–17	0.1.2, 0.1.4, 0.1.5, 0.1.6, 0.2.1, 0.2.4, 4.1.7, 4.6.1, 4.8.1, 4.8.2, 6.0.1, 7.1.1, 7.1.4, 7.2.1, 7.2.3, 7.2.4, 7.4.1, 7.5.1	▪ Asking and answering common questions ▪ Expressing basic needs ▪ Engaging in routine social conversations ▪ Reading simple material on familiar subjects ▪ Understanding simple and compound sentences in single or linked paragraphs ▪ Writing simple notes and messages ▪ Basic computer literacy
Unit 2 **At school** Pages 18–31	0.1.2, 0.1.4, 0.1.5, 0.2.1, 0.2.4, 2.3.1, 2.3.2, 4.1.2, 4.6.1, 4.8.1, 4.8.2, 6.0.1, 7.1.1, 7.1.2, 7.1.3, 7.1.4, 7.2.1, 7.2.2, 7.2.4, 7.2.6, 7.3.1, 7.3.2, 7.3.4, 7.4.1, 7.4.2, 7.5.1, 7.5.6	▪ Common words, simple phrases, and sentences ▪ Asking and answering common questions ▪ Expressing basic needs ▪ Engaging in routine social conversations ▪ Understanding simple and compound sentences in single or linked paragraphs ▪ Practicing writing with correct grammar ▪ Interpreting simple directions and schedules
Unit 3 **Friends and family** Pages 32–43	0.1.2, 0.1.3, 0.1.4, 0.1.5, 0.2.1, 0.2.3, 0.2.4, 1.4.1, 1.4.7, 1.7.4, 2.3.1, 2.3.2, 3.4.2, 4.8.1, 4.8.2, 4.8.4, 5.3.7, 5.6.1, 5.6.2, 6.0.1, 7.1.4, 7.2.1, 7.4.2, 7.5.1, 8.2.6, 8.3.2	▪ Common words, simple phrases, and sentences ▪ Asking and answering common questions ▪ Engaging in routine social conversations ▪ Reading simple material on familiar subjects ▪ Writing simple notes and messages ▪ Practicing writing with correct grammar ▪ Interpreting simple directions and schedules
Unit 4 **Health** Pages 44–57	0.1.2, 0.1.3, 0.1.5, 0.1.7, 0.2.4, 2.3.2, 3.1.1, 3.2.1, 3.3.3, 3.4.2, 3.5.2, 3.5.4, 3.5.5, 3.5.8, 3.5.9, 4.8.1, 6.0.1, 7.1.4, 7.2.1, 7.3.2, 7.4.1, 7.4.2, 7.5.1, 8.1.1, 8.2.1	▪ Asking and answering common questions ▪ Expressing basic needs ▪ Engaging in routine social conversations ▪ Expanding understanding of grammar ▪ Reading simple material ▪ Practicing writing with correct grammar ▪ Filling out simple forms
Unit 5 **Around town** Pages 58–69	0.1.2, 0.1.4, 0.1.5, 0.2.1, 0.2.4, 2.3.1, 2.3.2, 2.6.1, 2.6.2, 2.6.3, 2.7.6, 4.8.1, 6.0.1, 7.1.1, 7.1.2, 7.1.4, 7.2.1, 7.4.2, 7.4.3, 7.5.1	▪ Asking and answering common questions ▪ Engaging in routine social conversations ▪ Expanding understanding of grammar ▪ Writing simple notes and messages ▪ Practicing writing with correct grammar ▪ Filling out simple forms ▪ Basic computer literacy

All units of *Ventures 2ⁿᵈ Edition* meet most of the EFF content standards and provide overall BEST test preparation.
   The chart above lists areas of particular focus.
For more details and correlations to other state standards, go to: www.cambridge.org/myresourceroom

EFF	Florida Adult ESOL Low Intermediate	LAUSD ESL Low Intermediate Competencies
▪ Conveying ideas in writing ▪ Cooperating with others ▪ Listening actively ▪ Reading with understanding ▪ Speaking so others can understand ▪ Taking responsibility for learning ▪ Understanding and working with pictures	4.01.02, 4.01.03, 4.03.07, 4.03.10, 4.03.11, 4.03.13, 4.03.15	I. 1 II. 3 IV. 29 VIII. 48, 50, 51, 52
▪ Attending to oral information ▪ Guiding others ▪ Monitoring comprehension and adjusting reading strategies ▪ Paying attention to conventions of spoken English ▪ Solving problems ▪ Cooperating with others ▪ Speaking so others can understand	4.01.02, 4.01.04, 4.03.07, 4.03.10, 4.03.11, 4.03.13	II. 3, 6 VIII. 50, 51, 52 IX. 64
▪ Organizing and presenting information to serve the purpose, context, and audience ▪ Paying attention to conventions of spoken English ▪ Selecting appropriate reading strategies ▪ Solving problems ▪ Speaking so others can understand ▪ Testing out new learning in real-life applications ▪ Cooperating with others	4.01.02, 4.01.3, 4.03.01, 4.03.07, 4.03.10, 4.03.11, 4.03.15, 4.04.05, 4.05.02, 4.07.01	I. 1 II. 3, 41, 5a, 6, 9 IV. 23 VIII. 50, 51, 52
▪ Attending to oral information ▪ Conveying ideas in writing ▪ Listening actively ▪ Offering clear input on own interests and attitudes ▪ Paying attention to conventions of written English ▪ Speaking so others can understand ▪ Cooperating with others	4.01.02, 4.03.07, 4.03.10, 4.03.11, 4.05.01, 4.05.02	I. 2 II. 3 VI. 36, 38, 41 VIII. 50, 51, 52
▪ Attending to oral information ▪ Cooperating with others ▪ Listening actively ▪ Monitoring progress toward goals ▪ Paying attention to conventions of written English ▪ Reading with understanding ▪ Understanding and working with pictures ▪ Speaking so others can understand	4.01.02, 4.01.03, 4.01.04, 4.01.08, 4.02.08, 4.03.07, 4.03.10, 4.03.11, 4.03.13, 4.03.15	II. 3 VIII. 50, 51, 52

UNIT	CASAS Competencies	NRS Educational Functioning Level Descriptors *Oral BEST: 42–50 (SPL 4)* *BEST Plus: 439–472 (SPL 4)* *BEST Literacy: 47–53 (SPL 4)*
Unit 6 **Time** Pages 70–83	0.1.2, 0.1.4, 0.1.5, 0.2.1, 0.2.4, 1.1.3, 2.3.1, 2.7.2, 2.7.3, 4.1.7, 4.4.1, 4.4.3, 4.4.5, 4.8.1, 6.0.1, 6.7.4, 7.1.1, 7.1.2, 7.1.4, 7.2.1, 7.2.3, 7.2.4, 7.3.2, 7.4.1, 7.4.2, 7.4.8, 7.5.1	▪ Common words, simple phrases, and sentences ▪ Asking and answering common questions ▪ Engaging in routine social conversations ▪ Expanding understanding of grammar ▪ Reading simple material on familiar subjects ▪ Practicing writing with correct grammar ▪ Interpreting simple directions and schedules
Unit 7 **Shopping** Pages 84–95	0.1.2, 0.1.3, 0.1.5, 0.1.6, 0.2.1, 1.1.6, 1.2.1, 1.2.2, 1.2.5, 1.3.1, 1.4.1, 1.8.2, 4.8.1, 6.0.1, 6.5.1, 7.1.1, 7.1.4, 7.2.1, 7.2.3, 7.2.6, 7.3.1, 7.3.2, 7.4.2, 7.5.1, 7.5.5	▪ Common words, simple phrases, and sentences ▪ Engaging in routine social conversations ▪ Expanding understanding of grammar ▪ Understanding simple and compound sentences in single or linked paragraphs ▪ Writing simple notes and messages ▪ Practicing writing with correct grammar ▪ Interpreting simple directions and schedules
Unit 8 **Work** Pages 96-107	0.0.1, 0.1.2, 0.1.3, 0.1.5, 0.2.1, 2.3.1, 2.3.2, 2.4.1, 4.1.2, 4.1.5, 4.1.6, 4.1.7, 4.1.8, 4.4.3, 4.5.1, 4.6.1, 4.6.2, 4.8.1, 4.8.2, 6.0.1, 7.1.1, 7.1.4, 7.2.1, 7.4.1, 7.4.2, 7.4.4, 7.5.1, 7.5.2, 7.5.6	▪ Engaging in routine social conversations ▪ Expanding understanding of grammar ▪ Writing simple notes and messages ▪ Interpreting simple directions and schedules ▪ Practicing entry-level job-related writing ▪ Practicing entry-level job-related speaking ▪ Basic computer literacy
Unit 9 **Daily living** Pages 110–121	0.1.2, 0.1.4, 0.1.5, 0.2.1, 0.2.4, 1.4.1, 2.3.1, 2.5.1, 2.7.3, 3.4.2, 4.8.1, 5.3.7, 5.6.1, 5.6.2, 6.0.1, 7.1.1, 7.2.1, 7.4.2, 7.5.1, 8.3.2	▪ Common words, simple phrases, and sentences ▪ Asking and answering common questions ▪ Expressing basic needs ▪ Engaging in routine social conversations ▪ Expanding understanding of grammar ▪ Reading simple material on familiar subjects ▪ Practicing writing with correct grammar
Unit 10 **Free time** Pages 122–133	0.1.2, 0.1.4, 0.1.5, 0.2.1, 0.2.4, 1.2.2, 1.2.5, 2.1.8, 2.3.1, 2.3.2, 2.3.3, 2.7.1, 4.8.1, 6.0.1, 6.5.1, 7.1.1, 7.2.1, 7.2.2, 7.2.3, 7.2.6, 7.4.1, 7.4.2, 7.5.1	▪ Asking and answering common questions ▪ Engaging in routine social conversations ▪ Reading simple material on familiar subjects ▪ Understanding simple and compound sentences in single or linked paragraphs ▪ Practicing writing with correct grammar ▪ Interpreting simple directions and schedules ▪ Basic computer literacy

All units of *Ventures 2nd Edition* meet most of the EFF content standards and provide overall BEST test preparation. The chart above lists areas of particular focus.

For more details and correlations to other state standards, go to: www.cambridge.org/myresourceroom

EFF	Florida Adult ESOL Low Intermediate	LAUSD ESL Low Intermediate Competencies
■ Conveying ideas in writing ■ Cooperating with others ■ Listening actively ■ Reading with understanding ■ Solving problems ■ Speaking so others can understand	4.01.02, 4.01.5, 4.03.06, 4.03.07, 4.03.10, 4.03.11	II. 3 IV. 22 VIII. 50, 51, 52
■ Attending to oral information ■ Guiding others ■ Monitoring comprehension and adjusting reading strategies ■ Paying attention to conventions of written English ■ Selecting an alternative that is most appropriate to goal, context, and available resources ■ Understanding and working with pictures and numbers ■ Cooperating with others ■ Speaking so others can understand	4.01.02, 4.03.07, 4.03.10, 4.03.11, 4.04.01, 4.04.02, 4.04.03, 4.04.04, 4.04.07, 4.04.08, 4.04.09	II. 3, 5a IV. 23, 25c, 25d VIII. 49, 50, 51, 52
■ Anticipating and identifying problems ■ Conveying ideas in writing ■ Listening actively ■ Monitoring comprehension and adjusting reading strategies ■ Seeking input from others in order to understand their actions and reaction ■ Speaking so others can understand ■ Testing out new learning in real-life applications ■ Cooperating with others	4.01.02, 4.02.02, 4.02.06, 4.03.02, 4.03.04, 4.03.07, 4.03.10, 4.03.11, 4.03.13, 4.03.15	I. 1 II. 3, 4a, 5a VII. 44a VIII. 50, 51, 52
■ Attending to oral information ■ Monitoring progress toward goals ■ Paying attention to conventions of written English ■ Reading with understanding ■ Reflecting and evaluating ■ Taking responsibility for learning ■ Understanding and working with pictures and numbers ■ Cooperating with others ■ Speaking so others can understand	4.01.02, 4.02.05, 4.03.07, 4.03.10, 4.03.11, 4.06.04, 4.07.01	II. 3 IV. 23 VIII. 50, 51, 52
■ Attending to oral information ■ Interacting with others in ways that are friendly, courteous, and tactful ■ Listening actively ■ Monitoring comprehension and adjusting reading strategies ■ Paying attention to conventions of written English ■ Speaking so others can understand ■ Taking stock of where one is ■ Cooperating with others	4.01.02, 4.01.03, 4.03.07, 4.03.10, 4.03.11, 4.03.15, 4.04.03	II. 3 VIII. 50, 51, 52

Meet the *Ventures* author team

Gretchen Bitterlin has been an ESL teacher and an ESL department chair. She is currently the ESL coordinator for the Continuing Education Program at San Diego Community College District. Under Gretchen's leadership, the ESL program has developed several products – for example, an ESL oral interview placement test and writing rubrics for assessing writing for level exit – now used by other agencies. She is a co-author of *English for Adult Competency*, has been an item writer for CASAS tests, and chaired the task force that developed the TESOL *Adult Education Program Standards*. She is a recipient of her district's award, Outstanding Contract Faculty. Gretchen holds an MA in TESOL from the University of Arizona.

Dennis Johnson had his first language-teaching experience as a Peace Corps volunteer in South Korea. Following that teaching experience, he became an in-country ESL trainer. After returning to the United States, he became an ESL trainer and began teaching credit and non-credit ESL at City College of San Francisco. As ESL site coordinator, he has provided guidance to faculty in selecting textbooks. He is the author of *Get Up and Go* and co-author of *The Immigrant Experience*. Dennis is the demonstration teacher on the *Ventures Professional Development DVD*. Dennis holds an MA in music from Stanford University.

Donna Price began her ESL career teaching EFL in Madagascar. She is currently associate professor of ESL and vocational ESL / technology resource instructor for the Continuing Education Program, San Diego Community College District. She has served as an author and a trainer for CALPRO, the California Adult Literacy Professional Development Project, co-authoring training modules on contextualizing and integrating workforce skills into the ESL classroom. She is a recipient of the TESOL Newbury House Award for Excellence in Teaching, and she is author of *Skills for Success*. Donna holds an MA in linguistics from San Diego State University.

Sylvia Ramirez started as an instructional aide in ESL. Since then she has been a part-time teacher, a full-time teacher, and a program coordinator. As program coordinator at Mira Costa College, she provided leadership in establishing Managed Enrollment, Student Learning Outcomes, and Transitioning Adults to Academic and Career Preparation. Her more than forty years in adult ESL includes multilevel ESL, vocational ESL, family literacy, and distance learning. She has also provided technical assistance to local ESL programs for the California State Department of Education. In 2011 she received the Hayward Award in education. Her MA is in education / counseling from Point Loma University, and she has certificates in TESOL and in online teaching.

K. Lynn Savage first taught English in Japan. She began teaching ESL at City College of San Francisco in 1974, where she has taught all levels of non-credit ESL and has served as vocational ESL resource teacher. She has trained teachers for adult education programs around the country as well as abroad. She chaired the committee that developed *ESL Model Standards for Adult Education Programs* (California, 1992) and is the author, co-author, and editor of many ESL materials including *Crossroads Café, Teacher Training through Video, Parenting for Academic Success, Building Life Skills, Picture Stories, May I Help You?*, and *English That Works*. Lynn holds an MA in TESOL from Teachers College, Columbia University.

To the student

Welcome to **Ventures**! The dictionary says that "venture" means a risky or daring journey. Its meaning is similar to the word "adventure." Learning English is certainly a journey and an adventure. We hope that this book helps you in your journey of learning English to fulfill your goals. We believe that this book will prepare you for academic and career courses and give you the English skills you need to get a job or promotion, go to college, or communicate better in your community. The CDs, the Workbooks, and the free Internet practice on the Arcade will help you improve your English outside class. Setting your personal goals will also help. Take a few minutes and write down your goals below. Good luck in your studies!

The Author Team
Gretchen Bitterlin
Dennis Johnson
Donna Price
Sylvia Ramirez
K. Lynn Savage

My goals for studying English

1. My first goal for studying English:	Date: _____
2. My second goal for studying English:	Date: _____
3. My third goal for studying English:	Date: _____

Welcome

1 Meet your classmates

A Look at the pictures. What do you see?

B What are the people doing?

2 Goals

STUDENT TK 2
ULAGG GD I TK 2

A **Listen.** Silvia is talking about her goals with a classmate. Write the three steps that Silvia needs to take to reach her goals.

> **Main goal:** She ___*wants to open*___ her own beauty salon someday.
> 1. want / open
>
> **Steps to take to reach the goal:**
>
> First, she _____ to beauty school for two years. Second, she
> 2. need / go
>
> _____ an exam to get her license. Third, she _____ in a
> 3. need / take   4. need / work
>
> salon to get experience. She _____ a business owner in five years
> 5. hope / become
>
> because she _____ for anyone else.
> 6. not want / work

Listen again. Check your answers.

B **Work** with a partner. Talk about Vinh and Sofiya.

Name	Wants to . . .	Needs to . . .
Vinh	open a restaurant	1. learn to cook 2. take business classes 3. work in a restaurant
Sofiya	get a GED	1. improve her English 2. go to night school 3. take the GED test

> Vinh wants to open a restaurant. First, he needs
> to learn how to cook. Second, he needs to . . .

C **Talk** with a partner. Complete the chart. Ask and answer questions about goals.

I want to . . .	I need to . . .		
	1.	2.	3.

A What do you want to do? **B** I want to . . .	**A** What steps do you need to take? **B** First, I need to . . .

Share information with your classmates.

3 Verb tense review (present and present continuous)

STUDENT TK 3
CLASS CD1 TK 3

A Listen to each sentence. Check (✓) the correct column.

	Present	Present continuous		Present	Present continuous
1.	✓		6.		
2.			7.		
3.			8.		
4.			9.		
5.			10.		

Listen again. Check your answers.

B Read. Complete the story. Use the present or present continuous.

> Oksana Petrova _____ *is* _____ from Russia. She _____ in
>   1. be   2. live
>
> Philadelphia right now. She _____ at an elementary school. She
>   3. work
>
> _____ a job as a teacher's assistant. She _____ at the
>   4. have   5. work
>
> school right now. She _____ the students with math at the moment.
>   6. help
>
> Oksana _____ to become a teacher in the U.S. She
>   7. want
>
> _____ English every evening. She _____ to take
>   8. study   9. plan
>
> elementary education classes at the community college next year. She
>
> _____ her money right now, because college classes are very
>   10. save
>
> expensive. She also _____ for another part-time job. She
>   11. look
>
> _____ to pay her bills every month.
>   12. need

STUDENT TK 4
CLASS CD1 TK 4

Listen and check your answers.

C Talk with a partner. Ask and answer questions.

Every day	Every week	Right now	At the moment
What do you do every day?	What do you do every week?	What are you doing right now?	What are you studying at the moment?
Do you go to school every day?	Do you do homework every week?	Are you working right now?	Are you living in an apartment at the moment?

4 Verb tense review (past and future)

STUDENT TK 5
CLASS CD1 TK 5

A Listen to each sentence. Check (✓) the correct column.

	Past	Future		Past	Future
1.	✓		6.		
2.			7.		
3.			8.		
4.			9.		
5.			10.		

STUDENT TK 5
CLASS CD1 TK 5

B Listen again. Circle the time phrases you hear. Then write them in the correct column.

in 2005   last night   last year   next month   next year   soon

Past	Future
in 2005	

C Write. Complete the sentences. Use the past or future.

1. **A** When _____*did*_____ you _____*move*_____ to this city?
   (move)

   B I _____ here in 2011.
   (move)

2. **A** How long _____ you _____ here?
   (stay)

   B Maybe I _____ _____ here for one more year.
   (stay)

3. **A** Where _____ you _____ before you moved here?
   (live)

   B I _____ in Taiwan.
   (live)

4. **A** How long _____ you _____ English in the future?
   (study)

   B I _____ _____ English for two more years.
   (study)

STUDENT TK 6
CLASS CD1 TK 6

Listen and check your answers.

D Talk with your classmates. Ask and answer the questions.

1. When did you move to this city?
2. How long will you stay here?

3. Where did you live before you moved here?
4. How long will you study English?

LESSON A
Listening

1 **Before you listen**

A What do you see?

B What is happening?

C What's the story?

Unit Goals

Identify personality types

Describe likes and interests

Interpret personal ads

2 Listen

STUDENT TK 7
CLASS CD1 TK 7

A **Listen** and answer the questions.

1. Who are the speakers?

2. What are they talking about?

STUDENT TK 7
CLASS CD1 TK 7

B **Listen again.** Put a check (✓) under the correct name.

	Fernando	Danny
1. is tired this morning	✓	
2. likes staying home		✓
3. worked on his car		✓
4. is outgoing	✓	
5. went out with his girlfriend	✓	
6. wants a girlfriend		✓

3 After you listen

A **Read.** Complete the story.

alone	dislikes	going out	party animal
dance club	enjoys	outgoing	shy

Fernando and Danny are talking about their weekend. Fernando is a very friendly and __outgoing__ person. He __enjoy__ dancing. Last night, he went to a
  1   2
__party animal__ and stayed until late. Danny thinks Fernando is a __going out__.
  3   4

Danny is different from Fernando. He is __shy__ and quiet. He __dislike__
                                         5   6
dancing. Danny was home __alone__ the whole weekend. He likes staying at
                          7
home more than __dance club__. He wants a girlfriend who likes staying home, too.
                 8

STUDENT TK 8
CLASS CD1 TK 8

Listen and check your answers.

B **Talk** with a partner. Ask and answer the questions.

1. What are some things you enjoy doing on the weekend?

2. Are you outgoing or shy? Give some examples.

☑ Listen for activities and adjectives that describe personalities   **UNIT 1** **7**

LESSON B Verbs + gerunds

1 Grammar focus: questions and statements

Yes/No questions

Do you **enjoy dancing**?
Does he **like staying** home?

Short answers

Yes, I **do**.
No, he **doesn't**.

Statements

I **love dancing**.
He **hates staying** home.

Negatives

He **doesn't like dancing**.
I **don't mind staying** home.

Gerunds often follow these verbs:

dislike	hate	love
enjoy	like	mind

Turn to page 141 for a complete grammar chart and explanation.

USEFUL LANGUAGE

Do you mind? = Does it bother you?
I don't mind. = It doesn't bother me.
*** Don't say ~~I mind~~.**

2 Practice

A **Write.** Complete the sentences. Use gerunds.

be	get	listen	play
do	go	pay	shop

1. Does Katrina like _____*shopping*_____ for clothes online?
2. My brother enjoys _____ soccer.
3. Mrs. Tanaka doesn't mind _____ up early.
4. I love _____ to the birds in the morning.
5. Do you mind _____ to the movies by yourself?
6. Do you enjoy _____ alone?
7. Most people don't enjoy _____ bills every month.
8. Winston dislikes _____ English homework.

Listen and check your answers.

CLASS CD1 TK 9

B Talk with a partner. Ask and answer questions about the pictures. Use gerunds.

A Do Liz and Fred love working in the garden?
B Yes, they do. They love working in the garden.

A Does Karl enjoy taking out the garbage?
B No, he doesn't. He doesn't enjoy taking out the garbage.

Liz and Fred

Karl

Ramon

1. love / work in the garden

2. enjoy / take out the garbage

3. like / go to the beach

Kim

Nasim

Marissa and Ethan

4. dislike / stand in line

5. mind / work out

6. hate / eat vegetables

Write a sentence about each picture.

Liz and Fred love working in the garden.

3 Communicate

A Work in a small group. Ask and answer questions about the activities.

A Tam, do you like being alone?
B I don't mind it. What about you?

USEFUL LANGUAGE

Say *What about you?* OR *How about you?* to ask the same question someone asked you.

- be alone
- dance
- learn languages
- surf the Internet
- play sports
- read magazines
- talk on the phone
- exercise
- clean the house

B Share information about your classmates.

LESSON C Comparisons

Statements

I enjoy walking **more than** driving.
She likes cooking **less than** eating.
They enjoy singing **as much as** dancing.

Turn to page 147 for a complete grammar chart and explanation.

2 Practice

A Write. Complete the sentences. Use *more than*, *less than*, or *as much as*.

1. Sally enjoys cooking
   ___*more than*___ washing
   dishes.
2. Sally likes washing dishes
   _____ cooking.

3. Alfredo loves listening to music
   _____ playing an
   instrument.
4. Alfredo enjoys playing an instrument
   _____ listening to
   music.

5. Pam likes working
   _____ going
   to school.
6. Pam enjoys going to school
   _____ working.

7. Marta enjoys painting
   _____ jogging.
8. Marta likes jogging
   _____ painting.

Listen and check your answers.

B Work with a partner. Talk about the bar graph. Use *more than*, *less than*, and *as much as*.

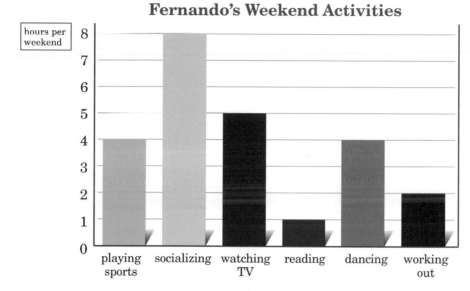

Fernando's Weekend Activities

A Fernando likes socializing more than reading.
B That's right.

USEFUL LANGUAGE

socializing = spending time with friends or family

1. socializing / reading
2. playing sports / dancing
3. socializing / working out
4. watching TV / socializing
5. reading / playing sports
6. working out / reading

Write sentences about Fernando's weekend activities.

Fernando enjoys socializing more than reading.

3 Communicate

A Work in a small group. Ask and answer questions about the activities in Exercise 2B.

Which do you like more, playing sports or socializing?

I like socializing more than playing sports.

B Share information about your classmates.

Amelia likes socializing more than playing sports.

LESSON **D** Reading

1 Before you read

Look at the reading tip. Answer the questions.

1. What jobs do the people in the pictures have?
2. What kind of person probably enjoys doing each job?
3. Look at the title and pictures to predict. What do you think the reading is about?

2 Read

Read the magazine article. Listen and read again.

STUDENT TK 9
CLASS CD1 TK 11

> Before you read, look at the title and the pictures. Predict, or guess, what you are going to read about. This will help you to read faster.

Your *Personality* and **Your Job**

What is the perfect job for you? It depends a lot on your personality. People think, act, and feel in different ways, and there are interesting jobs for every kind of person. Three common personality types are outgoing, intellectual, and creative.

Outgoing people enjoy meeting others and helping them. They are good talkers. They are friendly, and they get along well with other people. They often become nurses, counselors, teachers, or social workers.

Intellectual people like thinking about problems and finding answers to hard questions. They often enjoy reading and playing games like chess. Many intellectual people like working alone more than working in a group. They may become scientists, computer programmers, or writers.

Creative people enjoy making things. They like to imagine things that are new and different. Many of them become artists such as painters, dancers, or musicians. Architects, designers, and photographers are other examples of creative jobs.

Before you choose a career, think about your personality type. If you want to be happy in your work, choose the right job for your personality.

3 After you read

A Check your understanding.

1. What do outgoing people enjoy doing? What jobs are good for them?
2. What do intellectual people like doing? What jobs are good for them?
3. What do creative people enjoy doing? What jobs are good for them?
4. Why is it important for you to know your personality type?

B Build your vocabulary.

1. Find these words in the reading, and underline them.

artists   intellectual   personality

creative   outgoing   type

2. Find these phrases in the reading, and circle them.

enjoy meeting others   think, act, and feel in different ways

like to imagine things that are new and different   painters, dancers, or musicians

like thinking about problems   every kind of person

3. Look at the phrases in Exercise B2. They are clues to help you guess the meaning of these words. Write the phrases under the words.

   1. personality _think, act, and feel in different ways._

   2. type _every kind of person_

   3. outgoing _enjoy meeting others._

   4. intellectual _like thinking about problems._

   5. creative _like to imagine things that are new an different._

   6. artists _painters, dancers, or musicians._

4. Match the words and the definitions.

   1. personality _____   a. a kind of person or thing
   2. type _____   b. good at making things that are new and different
   3. outgoing _____   c. enjoys thinking and finding answers
   4. intellectual _____   d. a person who paints, dances, writes, or draws
   5. creative _____   e. the natural way a person thinks, feels, and acts
   6. artist _____   f. friendly

C Talk with a partner. Ask and answer the questions.

1. What personality type are you? Why do you think so?
2. What is a good job for you?

☑ Use the title and pictures to predict before you read; use clues to guess the meanings of words and phrases   **UNIT 1   13**

LESSON E Writing

1 Before you write

A **Work** in a small group. Think of adjectives that describe someone at work. Write them on the lines.

artistic	hard-working	honest	_____	_____
creative	highly-trained	patient	_____	_____
friendly	helpful	reliable	_____	_____

B **Talk** with a partner. Look at the pictures. Answer the questions.

1. What are these people doing? What are their jobs?
2. What are some adjectives that can describe these people?

a.

b.

c.

d.

e.

f.

C **Read** the paragraph.

Marcos
September 9

The Right Job

My sister, Leona, has the right job for her personality. She's a nurse. She works in a big hospital in the Philippines. Leona is a very outgoing person. She's very friendly with all her patients, and she enjoys talking to everybody in the hospital. She is warm and helpful. I think a nurse is a good job for her because it fits her personality.

Work with a partner. Answer the questions.

1. What does the first sentence say about Leona?
2. What is Leona's job?
3. Where does she work?
4. Leona is an outgoing person. Which sentences explain this?
5. Which adjectives describe Leona?
6. Is a nurse a good job for Leona? Why?

2 Write

Write a paragraph about the right job for someone you know. Describe the person and what he/she likes or enjoys. Use a topic sentence and supporting sentences. Use Exercises 1B and 1C to help you.

> A good paragraph is organized. Use a clear topic sentence and supporting sentences.

3 After you write

A **Check** your writing.

	Yes	No
1. I included a job and a personality type.	☐	☐
2. I described the person and what he/she likes or enjoys.	☐	☐
3. I used a topic sentence and supporting sentences.	☐	☐

B **Share** your writing with a partner.

1. Take turns. Read your paragraph to a partner.
2. Comment on your partner's paragraph. Ask your partner a question about the paragraph. Tell your partner one thing you learned.

LESSON F Another view

1 Life-skills reading

Fun-loving DM (46, 5'11", salt-and-pepper hair, N/S) enjoys taking motorcycle trips, camping outdoors, and spending time at the ocean. Seeking outgoing SF (40–50) for bike trips and fun.

Warm, kind, intelligent SM (27, 5'8") enjoys playing guitar, cooking, taking pictures. Seeking gentle SF (25–30) for musical evenings at home.

Caring SF (30, 5'5") loves playing tennis. Seeking good-looking, honest, active SM (28–35) with a good heart to share life together.

A Read the questions. Look at the Web page. Fill in the answer.

1. How tall is the man on the motorcycle?
   - Ⓐ under 5 feet
   - Ⓑ 5 feet 2 inches
   - ● 5 feet 11 inches
   - Ⓓ over 6 feet

2. What word describes the younger man?
   - Ⓐ friendly
   - Ⓑ fun-loving
   - Ⓒ honest
   - Ⓓ kind

3. What does the woman enjoy doing?
   - Ⓐ playing guitar
   - Ⓑ playing tennis
   - Ⓒ taking motorcycle trips
   - Ⓓ none of the above

4. Which ad talks about evenings at home?
   - Ⓐ the first ad
   - Ⓑ the second ad
   - Ⓒ the third ad
   - Ⓓ all of the above

B Talk with your classmates. Ask and answer the questions.

Is the Internet a good place to find a new friend? Why or why not?

2 Grammar connections: *must* for logical conclusions

Julia works until 11:00 p.m. every night.	→ She **must have** a difficult job. → She **must not eat** dinner at home.

A **Work** in a small group. Choose a situation and make conclusions. Take turns.

> **A** David's phone bill is usually over $200 a month.
> **B** He must talk on the phone a lot.
> **C** He must send a lot of texts, too.
> **D** He must not have a free Internet phone service.

1. David's phone bill is usually over $200 a month.
2. Susan gets up at 10:30 a.m. every morning.
3. Brenda buys a new car every year.
4. Sally spends a lot of time at the library.
5. Carlos goes to the gym five times a week.
6. George and Linda never cook at home.
7. Ivan doesn't have a computer.
8. Shawn and Olivia go to dance clubs a lot.

B **Talk** with a partner. Say something interesting about yourself. Your partner makes conclusions about you.

> **A** I went to 20 concerts last year.
> **B** You **must love** music.
> **A** Yes, I do. I love it!

3 Wrap up

Complete the **Self-assessment** on page 136.

LESSON A
Listening

1 Before you listen

A What do you see?

B What is happening?

C What's the story?

Unit Goals | **Identify** learning strategies
Relate learning strategies to study problems
Recognize test-taking strategies

UNIT 2

2 Listen

A **Listen** and answer the questions.

STUDENT TK 10
CLASS CD1 TK 12

1. Who are the speakers?　　2. What are they talking about?

B **Listen again.** Put a check (✓) next to Alex's study problems. Then write Bella's advice.

STUDENT TK 10
CLASS CD1 TK 12

Study problems	Bella's advice
1. ✓ too many things to do	*make a to-do list; do important things first*
2. ☐ always late for school	
3. ✓ can't concentrate	
4. ☐ can't pronounce English words	
5. ✓ can't remember vocabulary	

3 After you listen

A **Read.** Complete the story.

active　　boring　　concentrate　　discouraged　　index cards　　list　　paper

Alex has been at the library for a long time, and he is ___discouraged___. He has

many things to do. He needs to study for a test and write a ___paper___ [2]. He

needs to finish reading a book, but he can't ___concentrate___ [3]. He says the book is

___boring___ [4].

Alex's friend Bella gives him some study advice. First, she tells Alex to make

a ___list___ [5] of all the things he needs to do. Next, she says he has to be a

more ___active___ [6] reader. Finally, she tells him to write vocabulary words on

___index cards___ [7] and study them when he has free time. With Bella's help, Alex plans

to study smarter, not harder.

Listen and check your answers.

STUDENT TK 11
CLASS CD1 TK 13

B **Talk** with a partner. Ask and answer the questions.

1. What study problems do you have?　　2. What can you do to study better?

LESSON B Present perfect

1 Grammar focus: *how long, for, since*

Questions	Answers
How long has Alex **lived** here?	He **has lived** here **for** two years.
How long have you **known** Alex?	I **have known** him **since** January.

Past participles		Time phrases	
Regular verbs	**Irregular verbs**	for two hours	since 6:00 p.m.
live → lived	be → been	for one year	since February
wait → waited	have → had	for five months	since last year
work → worked	know → known		
	speak → spoken		
	teach → taught		

Turn to page 143 for a complete grammar chart and explanation.
Turn to page 146 for a list of irregular verbs.

2 Practice

A Write. Complete the sentences. Use the present perfect.

1. **A** How long _____ *has* _____ Manya _____ *been* _____ in the computer lab?
   (be)
   B Since six o'clock.

2. **A** How long _____ has _____ Avi _____ Known _____ Bella?
   (know)
   B For four months.

3. **A** How long _____ has _____ Kayla _____ worked _____ at the library?
   (work)
   B Since September.

4. **A** How long _____ has _____ Mrs. Bateson _____ taught _____ at the adult school?
   (teach)
   B For 20 years.

5. **A** How long _____ have _____ you _____ lived _____ in Canada?
   (live)
   B For one year.

6. **A** How long _____ has _____ Omar _____ had _____ two jobs?
   (have)
   B Since last year.

CLASS CD1 TK 14

Listen and check your answers. Then practice with a partner.

B **Talk** with a partner. Ask and answer questions about Alex. Use *since*.

> **A** How long has Alex been in the United States?
> **B** Since January 2012.

Alex's Recent History

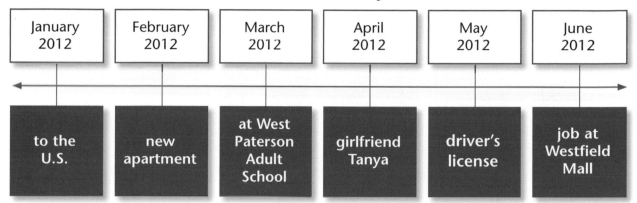

January 2012	February 2012	March 2012	April 2012	May 2012	June 2012
to the U.S.	new apartment	at West Paterson Adult School	girlfriend Tanya	driver's license	job at Westfield Mall

1. be in the U.S.
2. live in his new apartment
3. study at West Paterson Adult School
4. know his girlfriend Tanya
5. have a driver's license
6. work at Westfield Mall

Write today's date. Then write sentences about Alex. Use *for*.

Today is July 23, 2015.

Alex has been in the U.S. for three years and six months.

3 Communicate

A **Work** in a small group. Ask and answer questions with *how long*.

> **A** How long have you studied English?
> **B** For three years.
> **A** That's interesting. How long have you lived in this country?
> **B** Since 1998.
> **A** Wow!

USEFUL LANGUAGE
To express interest or surprise, you can say: *That's interesting.* *Really?* *Wow!*

1. study / English
2. live / in this country
3. be / at this school
4. work / in this country
5. have / your job
6. know / our teacher
7. be / married
8. lived / in your present home

B **Share** information about your classmates.

☑ Use the present perfect with *how long*, *for*, and *since*   UNIT 2   **21**

LESSON C Present perfect

1 **Grammar focus: questions with *ever*; short answers**

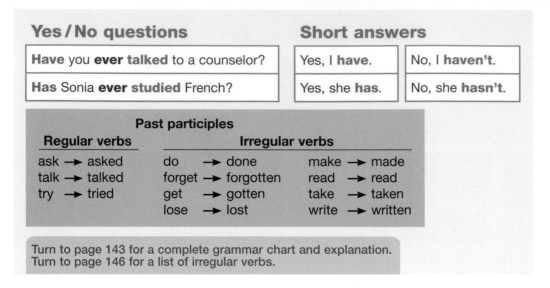

Yes / No questions	Short answers	
Have you **ever talked** to a counselor?	Yes, I **have**.	No, I **haven't**.
Has Sonia **ever studied** French?	Yes, she **has**.	No, she **hasn't**.

Past participles

Regular verbs	Irregular verbs	
ask → asked	do → done	make → made
talk → talked	forget → forgotten	read → read
try → tried	get → gotten	take → taken
	lose → lost	write → written

Turn to page 143 for a complete grammar chart and explanation.
Turn to page 146 for a list of irregular verbs.

2 **Practice**

A **Write.** Complete the sentences. Use *ever*.

> Check your past participle verb form. Use the chart on page 146.

1. A ___Has Laura ever talked___ to her school counselor?
   (Laura / talk)

   B No, she hasn't.

2. A Have you ever forgotten your teacher's name?
   (you / forget)

   B Yes, I have.

3. A Has Joseph ever read a book in English?
   (Joseph / read)

   B No, he hasn't. But he wants to.

4. A Have Mary and Paula ever been late to school?
   (Mary and Paula / be)

   B No, they haven't.

5. A Have you ever tried to speak English with your neighbors?
   (you / try)

   B Yes, I have.

6. A Has Tomas ever taken the wrong bus to school?
   (Tomas / take)

   B No, he hasn't.

Listen and check your answers. Then practice with a partner.

B **Talk** with a partner. Ask and answer questions about study habits.

> **A** Have you ever made a to-do list?
> **B** No, never.
> **A** Have you ever asked questions in class?
> **B** Yes, I have.

Reminder: Good study habits

- make a to-do list
- ask questions in class
- make vocabulary cards
- write notes in your book
- underline important information
- study with a friend

Write sentences about your partner.

Omar has never made a to-do list. He has asked questions in class.

3 Communicate

A **Work** in a small group. Ask and answer questions about study problems. Complete the chart.

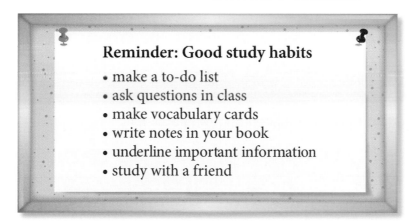

> **A** Have you ever had trouble concentrating?
> **B** Yes, I have.

forgotten
lost
done
been

Study problems	Name: Freddy	Name: Maria
have trouble concentrating	Yes	
forget to study for a test	Yes	Yes
lose your textbook	Yes	Yes
do the wrong homework	NO	Yes
be late to school	always	yes
(your idea)		

B **Share** information about your classmates. Give advice.

Ana has had trouble concentrating.

She should do her homework in a quiet place.

☑ Use the present perfect to ask and answer *Yes / No* questions with *ever* **UNIT 2** **23**

LESSON **D** Reading

1 Before you read

Look at the title and strategies. Answer the questions.

1. What is the reading about?
2. What are *strategies*?
3. How many strategies are there? What are they?

2 Read

Read the article from a student magazine. Listen and read again.

STUDENT TK 12
CLASS CD1 TK 16

Strategies for Learning English

Have you ever felt discouraged because it's hard to speak and understand English? Don't give up! Here are three strategies to help you learn faster and remember more.

Strategy #1 Set goals.

Have you ever set goals for learning English? When you set goals, you decide what you want to learn. After you determine your purpose for learning, you can make a plan to help you reach your goals. Maybe your goal is to learn more vocabulary. There are many ways to do this. For example, you can read in English for 15 minutes every day. You can also learn one new word every day.

Strategy #2 Look for opportunities to practice English.

Talk to everyone. Speak with people in the store, at work, and in the park. Don't worry about making mistakes. And don't forget to ask questions. For example, if your teacher uses a word you don't understand, ask a question like "What does that word mean?"

Strategy #3 Guess.

Don't try to translate every word. When you read, concentrate on clues such as pictures or other words in the sentence to help you understand. You can also make guesses when you are talking to people. For example, look at their faces and hand gestures – the way they move their hands – to help you guess the meaning.

Set goals, look for opportunities to practice, and guess. Do these things every day, and you will learn more English!

> In a reading, *for example* means *details will follow.*

3 After you read

A Check your understanding.

1. What are goals?
2. What is an example of setting goals?
3. What is an example of looking for opportunities to practice English?
4. You ask someone in line at a supermarket, "What time is it?" What strategy are you using?
5. If you read a story without using a dictionary, what clues help you guess?

B Build your vocabulary.

1. Look at the chart. Find the vocabulary words in the article. Underline them.
2. Use the context to decide the part of speech of each word – *noun* or *verb*. Write it in the chart.
3. Circle the best definition to match the part of speech.

Vocabulary	Part of speech	Definition
1. set	*verb*	a. a group of related things, such as dishes (b.) to choose or decide on something, such as a goal
2. plan		a. something you have decided to do b. to decide about something you want to do
3. practice		a. an activity you do to improve your ability b. to do something regularly to improve your ability
4. guess		a. an answer that you think is right, but you're not sure b. to give an answer that you think is right
5. clues		a. information you use to guess or solve problems b. to give someone useful information
6. pictures		a. paintings, drawings, or photographs b. to paint, draw, or photograph something
7. gestures		a. hand movements that have a special meaning b. to tell something by moving your hands

C Talk with a partner. Ask and answer the questions.

1. Have you ever set goals for learning English?
   What were they?
2. How do you practice something new?
   Give an example.
3. When you speak, what gestures do you use?

LESSON E Writing

1 Before you write

A Work in a small group. Complete the chart with examples of strategies for learning English. Use the reading on page 24 and your own ideas.

Strategy	Examples from reading	Your examples
Set goals.	*Read for 15 minutes in English every day.*	*Write in English every day for five minutes.*
Practice English.		
Guess.		

B Read the paragraph.

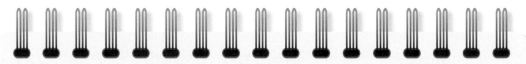

My Strategies for Learning English

There are two strategies I'm going to use to help me learn English. My first strategy is to learn more English vocabulary. There are many ways I will do this. For example, I'm going to learn one new English word every day. I'm also going to write my new words in a notebook. Another strategy I will use is looking for places to practice my English. For example, I'm going to talk to more English speakers at the store and at work. I can't wait to try these new strategies because I want to speak, read, and write English better.

Use examples to support your ideas.

Work with a partner. Answer the questions.

1. What is the writer's first strategy?
2. What examples does the writer give of the first strategy?
3. What is the writer's second strategy?
4. What example does the writer give of the second strategy?
5. The writer says, "I can't wait to try these new strategies." What does that mean?
6. Do you think these strategies could help you?

C **Write** a plan for a paragraph about strategies for learning English. Answer the questions.

1. What is one strategy you want to try?	
2. What is one example of this strategy?	
3. What is another strategy you want to try?	
4. What is one example of this strategy?	
5. Why do you want to try these strategies?	

2 Write

Write a paragraph about strategies for learning English. Include a topic sentence that focuses on strategies. Write about two strategies and give one or two examples for each one. Use Exercises 1B and 1C to help you.

3 After you write

A **Check** your writing.

	Yes	No
1. I included a topic sentence that focuses on strategies.	☐	☐
2. I wrote about two strategies I want to try.	☐	☐
3. I gave two examples for each strategy.	☐	☐

B **Share** your writing with a partner.

1. Take turns. Read your paragraph to a partner.
2. Comment on your partner's paragraph. Ask your partner a question about the paragraph. Tell your partner one thing you learned.

LESSON F Another view

1 Life-skills reading

Tips for Taking Tests

1 Read the instructions carefully. Ask the teacher if you don't understand them.

2 Skim the whole test before you begin. This will help you decide how to use your time.

3 Answer the easiest questions first.

4 Don't spend a lot of time on one question. Go back to it later if you have time.

5 Don't worry if other classmates finish before you. Pay attention to your own test.

6 Leave time to check your answers. Make sure you have answered every question.

7 Don't look at another student's paper. Be responsible for your own work.

> **CULTURE NOTE**
>
> During a test, don't look at another student's paper, ask another student for help, or help another student. These are types of cheating.

A Read the questions. Look at the tips. Fill in the answer.

1. Which tip says to read the whole test quickly before you answer any questions?

   (A) Tip 1   (C) Tip 6
   (B) Tip 2   (D) Tip 7

2. Which tip tells you to answer the questions you know first?

   (A) Tip 1   (C) Tip 3
   (B) Tip 2   (D) Tip 4

3. Which tip tells you to skip the questions you don't know and go back to them later?

   (A) Tip 3   (C) Tip 5
   (B) Tip 4   (D) Tip 6

4. Which tip says you should answer every question?

   (A) Tip 1   (C) Tip 4
   (B) Tip 3   (D) Tip 6

B Talk with a partner. Ask and answer the questions.

1. Have you ever tried any of these tips? Did they help you?
2. Do you have any other tips for taking tests? What are they?

2 Grammar connections: simple past and present perfect

Use the *simple past* for an activity that happened at a specific time in the past.	Use the *present perfect* for an activity that began in the past and continues to the present.
She **studied** Spanish in 2011.	She **has studied** Spanish for ten years.

A **Talk** with a partner. You need an English tutor. Look at the chart and compare the two tutors. Use the simple past and present perfect to talk about the tutors' experience. With your partner, choose the tutor you think is best.

A Rita would be a good tutor. She studied Spanish for four years, and she took French classes. She has also studied Arabic since 2010.

B Maybe, but she hasn't had any tutoring experience. Dao has tutored English since 2011. He also . . .

Rita Lawrence

1950 – 1970	live in Phoenix, AZ
1970 – 1974	study Spanish in college
1974	graduate from college with B average, degree in education
1974 – 1980	teach English in Mexico
1981	get married to English teacher
1982 – 2006	stay home with children
2006 – 2009	study French at night school
2006 – now	teach at an elementary school
2010 – now	study Arabic online
2011 – now	volunteer at a hospital translating Spanish to English

Dao Lin

1985 – 1999	live in Shanghai, China
1999	move to Chicago, IL
1999 – 2003	learn English in high school
2003 – 2007	study English and computer science in college
2007	graduate from college with A average, degree in computer science
2007	travel around U.S. for four months
2007 – 2009	work for travel agency
2010 – now	work as a computer technician
2011 – now	tutor English at a high school
2012 – now	live with aunt and uncle, who only speak Chinese

B **Share** your decision with the class.

We chose Rita because . . .

We chose Dao because . . .

3 Wrap up

Complete the **Self-assessment** on page 136.

☑ Scan a tip sheet to identify test-taking strategies; contrast simple past and present perfect

Review

CLASS CD1 TK 17

Listen. Put a check (✓) under the correct name.

	Vladimir	Marisol
1. asks the teacher questions		✓
2. asks another student questions		
3. writes vocabulary on index cards		
4. talks to co-workers		
5. is shy		
6. is outgoing		

Talk with a partner. Check your answers.

2 Grammar

A Write. Complete the story. Use the correct words.

Homework Problems

Jameela _____*has had*_____ a lot of problems with her son, Faisal, for
   1. has / has had
the past two months. He doesn't enjoy _____ science. He
                                         2. studying / study
_____ bad grades on his tests. The teacher said that Faisal
   3. get / has gotten
_____ his homework since December. Faisal said he hates
   4. doesn't do / hasn't done
_____ his science homework because he doesn't understand it.
   5. do / doing
Jameela _____ overtime at her job for the past two months, so she
   6. works / has worked
_____ able to help him. What should Jameela and her son do?
   7. hasn't been / won't be

B Write. Look at the answers. Write the questions.

1. **A** How long _has Jameela had problems with her son_____?
   B Jameela has had problems with her son for the past two months.

2. **A** _____ ever _____?
   B Yes, he has. Faisal has gotten bad grades on his tests for the past two months.

3. **A** How long _____?
   B Jameela has worked overtime for the past two months.

Talk with a partner. Ask and answer the questions.

3 Pronunciation: stressing content words

CLASS CD1 TK 18

A **Listen** to the stressed content words in each sentence. Content words include main verbs, nouns, adverbs, adjectives, and question words.

1. She <u>loves</u> <u>playing</u> <u>cards</u> with <u>friends</u>.
2. He <u>hates</u> <u>working</u> <u>in</u> the <u>garden</u>
3. Do you <u>like</u> <u>being</u> <u>alone</u>?
4. She <u>enjoys</u> <u>cooking</u> less than <u>eating</u>.
5. I <u>like</u> <u>living</u> in the <u>city</u>.
6. <u>How</u> <u>long</u> has Shen <u>studied</u> <u>English</u>?
7. He's been <u>here</u> for <u>six</u> <u>months</u>.
8. Have you <u>ever</u> <u>studied</u> <u>Korean</u>?

Listen again and repeat. Stress the content words.

CLASS CD1 TK 19

B **Listen and repeat.** Then underline the content words.

1. <u>What</u> is the <u>perfect</u> <u>job</u> for you?
2. The perfect job depends on your personality.
3. Have you ever felt discouraged?
4. Have you ever set goals for learning English?
5. What does that word mean?
6. Intellectual people often enjoy working alone.

Read your sentences to a partner. Compare your answers.

C **Read** the paragraph. Underline the content words.

My sister has the right job for her personality. She's a nurse. She works in a big hospital in the Philippines. She is a very outgoing person. She's very friendly with all her patients, and she enjoys talking to people in the hospital. She is warm and helpful. I think a nurse is a good job for her because it fits her personality.

Talk with a partner. Compare your answers. Read the paragraph to your partner. Stress the content words.

LESSON A
Listening

1 Before you listen

A What do you see?

B What is happening?

C What's the story?

Unit Goals	**Describe** a housing problem
	Read an article in a newsletter about Neighborhood Watch
	Write a letter of complaint

2 Listen

STUDENT TK 13
CLASS CD1 TK 20

A **Listen** and answer the questions.

1. Who are the speakers?   2. What are they talking about?

STUDENT TK 13
CLASS CD1 TK 20

B **Listen again.** Put a check (✓) next to Ana's problems.

1. ☑ been busy   4. ☐ car alarm broken
2. ☐ children sick   5. ☑ smoke alarm needs battery
3. ☐ ceiling is too high   6. ☑ neighbors are noisy

3 After you listen

A **Read.** Complete the story.

appreciates	come over	favor	noisy
borrow	complain	noise	owe

[handwritten: ruidoso/sa over "noisy"; ruido over "noise"; deber over "owe"; ower, poder]

Ana and Maria are neighbors. Ana calls Maria because she needs a ___favor___.
                                                                            1
The smoke alarm in Ana's kitchen is beeping. She needs to change the battery, but

the ceiling in her kitchen is too high. Ana asks to ___borrow___ Maria's ladder.
                                                          2

Maria says her husband, Daniel, will ___come over___ with a ladder and help Ana.
                                            3
Ana says, "I ___owe___ you one." This means she ___appreciates___ Maria and
              4   5
Daniel's help, and she will do a favor for them in the future.

Next, Maria tells Ana about their ___noise___ neighbors. The neighbors had a
                                          6
party on Saturday night. Because of the ___noisy___, Maria and Daniel couldn't
                                               7
sleep. Ana tells Maria that she should ___complain___ to the apartment manager.
                                              8

STUDENT TK 14
CLASS CD1 TK 21

Listen and check your answers.

B **Talk** with a partner. Ask and answer the questions.

1. Have you ever borrowed something from a neighbor? What did you borrow?
2. Have you ever lent something to a neighbor? What did you lend?

> **USEFUL** LANGUAGE
>
> When you *lend* something *to* someone, you give it for a short time. When you *borrow* something *from* someone, you receive it.

☑ Listen for and identify a housing problem   **UNIT 3**   **33**

LESSON B Phrases and clauses with *because*

1 Grammar focus: *because of* phrases and *because* clauses

porque

because of + noun phrase
Ana can't reach the smoke alarm **because of** the high ceiling.
Because of the high ceiling, Ana can't reach the smoke alarm.

porque

because + clause
Ana can't reach the smoke alarm **because** the ceiling is too high.
Because the ceiling is too high, Ana can't reach the smoke alarm.

Turn to page 147 for a grammar explanation.

Turn to page 147 for a grammar explanation.

> **USEFUL LANGUAGE**
>
> When you read aloud, pause when you see a comma.
> *Because of the high ceiling,* (pause) *Ana can't reach the smoke alarm.*

2 Practice

A Write. Complete the sentences. Use *because* or *because of*.

A Nice Surprise

Lei wanted to bake a cake _____because_____ it was her
                  1

neighbor Margy's birthday. Lei needed to go to the store

_____because_____ she didn't have any flour. However, her
      2

car had a flat tire. _because of_ this problem, she couldn't drive to the store. She
       3

couldn't walk to the store _because of_ the distance. It was more than a mile away.
       4

Lei had a clever idea. She went to Margy and asked to borrow a cup of flour. Margy

was happy to help _because_ she had a lot of flour and she was a good neighbor.
      5

Two hours later, Lei returned to Margy's house with a beautiful cake. When Margy

opened the door, Lei shouted, "Happy birthday!" Margy was very surprised and happy.

because of the nice surprise, Margy had a wonderful birthday!
 6

🎧 **Listen** and check your answers.

B . **Talk** with a partner. Ask and answer questions about the problems.

> **A** Why couldn't you sleep last night?
> **B** Because of my noisy neighbors.

Problem	Reason
1. You couldn't sleep last night.	noisy neighbors
2. You couldn't make a cake.	didn't have any eggs
3. The neighbors couldn't lock the door.	lock was broken
4. You couldn't change the alarm battery.	didn't have a ladder
5. The children couldn't play outside.	the rain
6. You couldn't come to school.	car had a flat tire

Write a sentence about each problem.

I couldn't sleep last night because of my noisy neighbors.

3 Communicate

A **Work** in a small group. Ask and answer questions. Complete the chart.

> **A** Why did you come to this country, Shakir?
> **B** Because of my children. They live here.
> **A** Why do you live in your neighborhood?
> **B** Because it's close to my job.

Name	Why did you come to this country?	Why do you live in your neighborhood?
Shakir	children live here	close to job

B **Share** information about your classmates.

☑ Use *because* and *because of* to give reasons **UNIT 3** **35**

LESSON C Adverbs of degree

1 Grammar focus: *too* and *enough*

too + adjective

The ceiling is **too high**.
It's **too high** to reach.

Adjective + *enough*

The ladder is **tall enough**.
It's **tall enough** to reach the ceiling.

not + adjective + *enough*

The woman is **not tall enough**.
She is **not tall enough** to reach the ceiling.

Adjectives		
big	expensive	far
close	experienced	high

Use the shorter sentence when the listener knows what you are talking about. Example: *The ladder is tall enough.*

Turn to page 147 for a grammar explanation.

2 Practice

A Write. Complete the sentences. Use *too* or *enough*.

Too Far to Visit

My neighbors – the Mansours – have four children. Their house isn't big _____. Mr. and Mrs. Mansour think it's
1
_____ expensive to live in the city. Their rent is
2
_____ high. Last weekend, the Mansours bought a
3
house outside the city. It has four bedrooms. It's big
_____ for the whole family. However, the new house is
4
_____ far from Mr. Mansour's job, so he's going to look for a new job.
5
Mr. Mansour is an experienced engineer. He's
experienced _____ to find a new job.
6
I will miss the Mansours. I probably can't
visit them. Their new house isn't close
_____ for me to visit.
7

Listen and check your answers.

CLASS CD1 TK 23

B **Work** with a partner. Talk about the pictures. Use *too*, *enough*, and *not . . . enough*.

A Can they swim today?
B I don't think so. It's too cold to swim today.
A Yeah, you're right. It really isn't warm enough.

A Can she swim today?
B Yes, it's hot enough to swim.

1. cold / swim / warm

2. hot / swim

3. young / drive / old

4. old / drive

5. weak / lift the TV / strong

6. strong / lift the TV

Write sentences about each picture.

It's too cold to swim.

It isn't warm enough to swim.

USEFUL LANGUAGE

I agree. = My opinion is the same as yours.

I disagree. / I don't agree. = My opinion is different from yours.

3 **Communicate**

Work in a small group. Talk about what you are *too young*, *too old*, *young enough*, or *old enough* to do. Give your opinions.

I'm too young to get married.

I agree. Young people should wait to get married.

☑ Use *enough* and *too* UNIT 3 **37**

LESSON **D** Reading

1 Before you read

Look at the title and the picture. Answer the questions.

1. Have you ever heard of Neighborhood Watch? What is it?
2. Is there a Neighborhood Watch in your area?

2 Read

STUDENT TK 15
CLASS CD1 TK 24

Read the article from a neighborhood newsletter. **Listen and read again.**

> The first sentence of a paragraph usually tells the main idea. The other sentences give details. Facts and examples are types of details.

Neighborhood Watch Success Story

by Latisha Holmes, President, Rolling Hills Neighborhood Watch

People often ask me about the role of Neighborhood Watch. My answer is *Because of Neighborhood Watch, our neighborhood is safer and nicer.* Members of Neighborhood Watch help each other and look after the neighborhood. For example, we look after our neighbors' houses when they aren't home. We help elderly neighbors with yard work. Once a month, we get together to paint over graffiti.

Last Wednesday, the Neighborhood Watch team had another success story. Around 8:30 p.m., members of our Neighborhood Watch were out on a walk. Near the Corner Café, they noticed two men next to George Garcia's car. George lives on Rolling Hills Drive. The men were trying to break into the car. Suddenly, the car alarm went off. The men ran away and got into a car down the street. But they weren't quick enough. Our Neighborhood Watch members wrote down the car's license plate number and called the police. Later that night, the police arrested the two men.

I would like to congratulate our Neighborhood Watch team on their good work. Because so many people participate in Neighborhood Watch, Rolling Hills is a safer neighborhood today.

For information about Neighborhood Watch, please call 773-555-1234.

3 After you read

A **Check** your understanding.

1. What is the main idea of the first paragraph?
2. What are three examples of the role of Neighborhood Watch?
3. Does the second paragraph give facts or examples?
4. What did the Neighborhood Watch team see? What did they do?

B **Build** your vocabulary

1. Read the dictionary entry for the word *get*. Find the definition of *get together*.

> **get** /get/ [T] **getting**, *past* **got**, *past part* **gotten** to take (something)
>   into your possession
>   **get together** *v/adv* [I/T] to meet; to have a meeting or party

2. *Get together* is a two-word verb. Look at the article in Exercise 2. Match the two-word verbs.

   get   look   break   run   get   go

   after   into   together   into   away   off

3. Write each verb in Exercise B2 next to its definition.

1. to meet	*get together*
2. to enter (a car legally)	
3. to enter (a car illegally)	
4. to make a sudden, loud noise	
5. to escape; to leave a place very fast	
6. to take care of	

4. Complete the sentences with the verbs in Exercise B3.

   a. Let's _____*get together*_____ for coffee tomorrow, OK?
   b. Somebody tried to _____ my neighbor's house.
   c. I saw the girl next door _____ a car and drive away.
   d. My cats always _____ when the door is open.
   e. My neighbor's car alarm _____ at 3:00 a.m. every morning.
   f. All the people on my street _____ each other's houses.

C **Talk** with a partner. Ask and answer the questions.

1. Do you enjoy getting together with friends? What do you do?
2. Do you and your neighbors look after each other? How?

LESSON **E** Writing

1 Before you write

A **Talk** with a partner. Answer the questions.

1. Have you ever complained to your landlord or apartment manager?
2. What was the problem?
3. How did you complain – in person, by telephone, or in writing?
4. What happened?

B **Read** the letter of complaint.

LUIS RAMOS

January 14, 2013

Acme Properties
100 25th Avenue
New York, NY 10011

To Whom It May Concern:

My name is Luis Ramos. I live at 156 South
Flower Street, Apartment 3. I am writing
because my neighbors in Apartment 9 are too
noisy. I asked them to be quiet, but they still
have loud parties almost every night. Because
of the noise, my children can't sleep.

Can you please tell them to be quiet? I hope
you will take care of this as soon as possible.

Thank you in advance.

Sincerely,

Luis Ramos

> **CULTURE** NOTE
>
> When you don't know the
> name of the person you
> are writing to, use
> *To Whom It May Concern.*

Work with a partner. Answer the questions.

1. What is the date of the letter?
2. Who is the letter to?
3. Does the writer know the person's name?
4. Who wrote the letter?
5. What is the problem?
6. What does the writer want Acme Properties to do?

C Complete the letter of complaint.

advance	because	because of	sincerely	soon	very

To Whom It May Concern:

My name is Alina Krasinski. I live at 156 South Flower Street,

Apartment 6. I am writing ___because___ the pipes under my kitchen
                              1

sink are leaking. _____ the leak, my water bill will be
                        2

_____ high next month. The water is also bad for the kitchen
      3

floor. Can you please come as _____ as possible to fix the leak?
                                    4

Thank you in _____.
                  5

_____,
      6

Alina Krasinski

> A letter of complaint should include:
> • the problem
> • examples
> • a request to fix the problem

D Talk with your classmates. What housing problems do people complain about?

2 Write

Write a letter of complaint. Use *To Whom It May Concern* or the person's name. Include the problem, an example, and a request to fix the problem. Use the letters in Exercises 1B and 1C to help you.

3 After you write

A Check your writing.

	Yes	No
1. I used *To Whom It May Concern* or the person's name.	☐	☐
2. I included the problem and an example.	☐	☐
3. I included a request to fix the problem.	☐	☐

B Share your writing with a partner.

1. Take turns. Read your letter to a partner.
2. Comment on your partner's letter. Ask your partner a question about the letter. Tell your partner one thing you learned.

LESSON F Another view

1 Life-skills reading

Community Center Volunteers Needed	HOME ABOUT US CONTACT US

Organization:	Oak Park Community Center
Volunteers needed:	10
Date:	Open
Time:	9:00 a.m. – 10:00 p.m.
Estimated time:	4 hours per day
Location:	15 Franklin Street Dallas, TX 75231
Description:	1. Volunteers to provide food and drinks to visitors 2. Volunteers for theater to greet people, answer questions, assist with seating 3. Volunteers for Arts Program to assist teachers with classes
Requirements:	Reliable; teamwork skills; good customer service Prefer 18 years old and over

A Read the questions. Look at the ad. Fill in the answer.

1. How many volunteers does the center need?
   - Ⓐ four
   - Ⓑ five
   - Ⓒ ten
   - Ⓓ twenty

2. What can a volunteer do at this center?
   - Ⓐ greet people
   - Ⓑ help the art teachers
   - Ⓒ serve food
   - Ⓓ all of the above

3. How long do volunteers need to work?
   - Ⓐ one hour a day
   - Ⓑ four hours a day
   - Ⓒ eight hours a day
   - Ⓓ nine hours a day

4. Which statement is true?
   - Ⓐ Volunteers must be artists.
   - Ⓑ Volunteers must be experienced cooks.
   - Ⓒ Volunteers must be over 21 years old.
   - Ⓓ Volunteers must be team players.

B Talk with your classmates. Ask and answer the questions.

1. Have you ever volunteered in your community?
2. If yes, what did you do?

2 Grammar connections: *be able to*

> **Use *be able to* for ability.**
>
> | I'm **able to drive**. | Isabel **isn't able to drive**. |
> |---|---|

 = 1 space

 = 2 spaces

A **Work** in a small group. Play the game. Write your name on a small piece of paper. Flip a coin to move your paper. Then tell your group about the topic in the square. Use *be able to* in your answer. Take turns.

> **A** This says, "A food you are able to make in less than 15 minutes." OK. I'm able to make cookies in less than 15 minutes.
>
> **B** My space says, "Something you aren't able to lift." I'm not able to lift my nephew! He's ten years old and very heavy!

Start here → A food you are able to make in less than 15 minutes → Something you aren't able to lift → Someone you know who isn't able to drive

A sport you aren't able to do well ← Someone you know who is able to play a musical instrument ← Something you aren't able to do while you're talking ← An animal that isn't able to swim

A non-food item you are able to buy at a supermarket → Something you are able to do with one hand → A language you are able to speak well → Someone you know who isn't able to sing well

Finish! ← Something you are able to do in a swimming pool ← Something you aren't able to cook ← A sport you are able to do well

B **Share** information about your classmates.

> Katia is able to make cookies in less than 15 minutes.

> Carlos isn't able to lift his nephew.

3 Wrap up

Complete the **Self-assessment** on page 137.

☑ Interpret an ad for volunteers; use *be able to* for ability   **UNIT 3**   **43**

LESSON A
Listening

1 **Before you listen**

A What do you see?

B What is happening?

C What's the story?

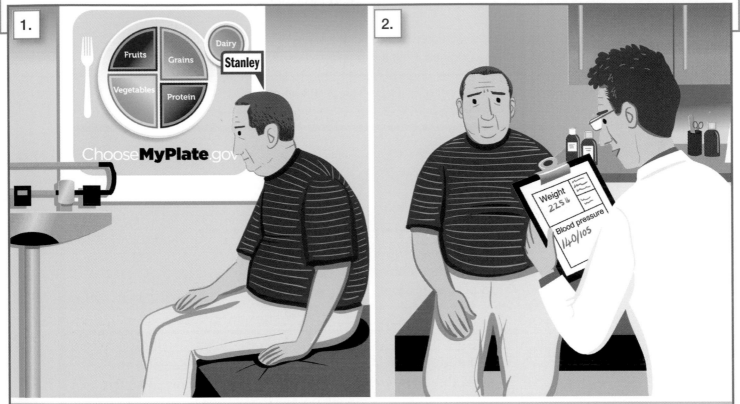

Unit Goals	**Recognize** good health habits
	Describe beneficial plants
	Complete a medical history form

UNIT 4

2 Listen

STUDENT TK 16
CLASS CD1 TK 25

A **Listen** and answer the questions.

1. Who are the speakers?
2. What are they talking about?

STUDENT TK 16
CLASS CD1 TK 25

B **Listen again.** Put a check (✓) next to the doctor's advice.

1. ☐ sleep more   5. ☐ eat hamburgers
2. ☑ take a walk every day   6. ☐ eat breakfast
3. ☐ ride a bicycle   7. ☐ eat fish
4. ☐ take the elevator at work 8. ☐ take medication

3 After you listen

A **Complete** the story.

advice	exercise	medication	tired
diet	health	pressure	weight

Stanley is at the doctor's office. His _____health_____ has always been good, but he
                                          1
has been really _____ lately. The doctor looks at Stanley's chart. He sees
                      2
a couple of problems. One problem is Stanley's _____. He has gained 20
                                                      3
pounds. Another problem is his blood _____. The doctor tells him he needs
                                            4
regular _____ – for example, walking or riding a bike. He also tells Stanley
             5
to change his _____ – to eat more fish and vegetables. If Stanley doesn't do
                    6
these things, he will need to take pills and other _____. Stanley wants to be
                                                          7
healthy, so he is going to try to follow the doctor's _____.
                                                            8

STUDENT TK 17
CLASS CD1 TK 26

Listen and check your answers.

B **Talk** with a partner. Ask and answer the question.

What are three things you do to stay healthy?

LESSON B Present perfect

1 **Grammar focus:** *recently* and *lately*

Questions	Statements
Have you **gained** weight **recently**?	I **have gained** weight **recently**.
Has Sheila **gone** to the gym **lately**?	Sheila **hasn't gone** to the gym **lately**.

Past participles

Regular verbs		Irregular verbs	
check → checked	start → started	eat → eaten	lose → lost
exercise → exercised	visit → visited	give → given	see → seen
gain → gained	weigh → weighed	go → gone	sleep → slept

Turn to page 143 for a complete grammar chart and explanation.
Turn to page 146 for a list of irregular verbs.

2 **Practice**

A **Write.** Complete the sentences. Use the present perfect.

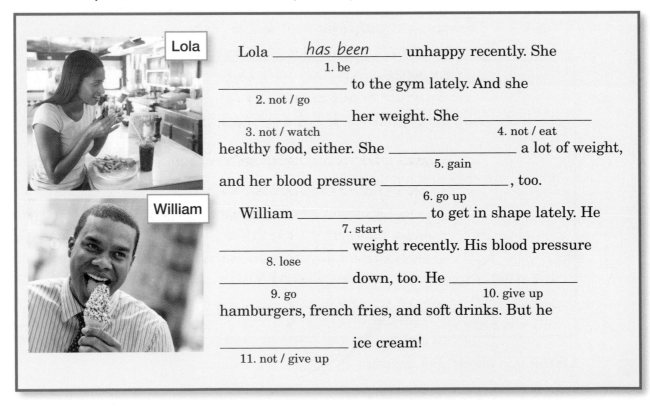

Lola

Lola _____*has been*_____ unhappy recently. She
    1. be
_____ to the gym lately. And she
    2. not / go
_____ her weight. She _____
    3. not / watch   4. not / eat
healthy food, either. She _____ a lot of weight,
                              5. gain
and her blood pressure _____, too.
                            6. go up
    William _____ to get in shape lately. He
              7. start
_____ weight recently. His blood pressure
    8. lose
_____ down, too. He _____
    9. go   10. give up
hamburgers, french fries, and soft drinks. But he

_____ ice cream!
    11. not / give up

William

Listen and check your answers.

CLASS CD1 TK 27

B **Talk** with a partner. Ask and answer questions. Use the present perfect with *recently* and *lately*.

A Has Elisa lost weight recently? **B** Yes, she has.	**A** Has Roberto given up desserts lately? **B** No, he hasn't.

1. Elisa / lose weight 2. Roberto / give up desserts 3. Joy / start taking vitamins

4. Ahmet / gain weight 5. Martin and Julie / start exercising a lot 6. Lee / sleep much

Write a sentence about each picture. Use the present perfect with *recently* and *lately*.

Elisa has lost weight recently.

3 Communicate

A **Work** with a partner. Ask and answer questions. Complete the chart.

A Have you eaten a lot of fish lately? **B** Yes, I have. How about you?	**A** Have you had a cold lately? **B** No, I haven't. What about you?

Partner's name: _____	Yes	No
1. eat a lot of fish		
2. have a cold		
3. check your blood pressure		
4. see a doctor		
5. go to the gym		
6. visit a dentist		

B **Share** information about your partner.

LESSON C *Used to*

1 Grammar focus: statements and questions

Statements	Yes / No questions	Short answers
I **used to** eat a lot of fatty foods.	**Did** you **use to** eat a lot of fatty foods?	Yes, I did.
She **didn't use to** go to bed late.	**Did** she **use to** go to bed late?	No, she didn't.

Turn to page 144 for a complete grammar chart and explanation.

2 Practice

A Write. Complete the sentences. Use *use to* or *used to*.

1. **A** Did he _____*use to*_____ stay up all night?
   B Yes, he did, but he goes to bed early now.

2. **A** How often do you eat meat?
   B I _____ eat meat every night, but now I usually have fish.

3. **A** Did you _____ drive to work?
   B Yes, I did, but now I ride my bike.

4. **A** What do you usually do after work?
   B We _____ go straight home, but now we take dance classes twice a week.

5. **A** Do you exercise every day?
   B I _____ exercise every day, but now I exercise only on weekends.

Listen and check your answers. Then practice with a partner.

CLASS CD1 TK 28

B **Work** with a partner. Talk about Michael as a young man and Michael today.

> Michael used to play sports, but he doesn't anymore. Now he watches sports on TV.

When Michael was young	Michael now
1. play sports	watch sports on TV
2. skip breakfast	eat three meals a day
3. take vitamins	not take vitamins
4. drink coffee	drink tea
5. sleep late	get up early
6. eat fruit between meals	eat candy and chips between meals
7. work out every afternoon	take a nap every afternoon

Write sentences about Michael.

When Michael was young, he used to play sports. Now he watches sports on TV.

3 Communicate

A **Work** in a small group. Complete the sentences. Talk about your health habits.

1. When I was a child, I used to . . . , but now I . . .
2. In my country, I used to . . . , but now I . . .
3. When I was a teenager, I used to . . . , but now I . . .
4. When I first came to this country, I used to . . . , but now I . . .
5. When I had more time, I used to . . . , but now I . . .

B **Share** information about your classmates.

LESSON D Reading

1 Before you read

Look at the reading tip. Then read the first and last paragraphs. Answer the questions.

1. Which two plants is the reading about?
2. How long have people used them?

USEFUL LANGUAGE

Use *beneficial* to describe something that's good for you.

2 Read

Read the magazine article. Listen and read again.

STUDENT TK 18
CLASS CD1 TK 29

The first paragraph of a reading is the **introduction**. It tells you the topic. The last paragraph is the **conclusion**. It often repeats the topic with different words.

Two Beneficial Plants

Since the beginning of history, people in every culture have used plants to stay healthy and to prevent sickness. Garlic and chamomile are two beneficial plants.

Garlic is a plant in the onion family. The green stem and the leaves of the garlic plant grow above the ground. The root – the part under the ground – is a bulb with sections called cloves. They look like the pieces of an orange. The bulb is the part that people have traditionally used for medicine. They have used it for insect bites, cuts, earaches, and coughs. Today, some people also use it to treat high blood pressure and high cholesterol.

Chamomile is a small, pretty plant with flowers that bloom from late summer to early fall. The flowers have white petals and a yellow center. Many people use dried chamomile flowers to make tea. Some people give the tea to babies with upset stomachs. They also drink chamomile tea to feel better when they have a cold or the flu, poor digestion, or trouble falling asleep.

For thousands of years, people everywhere have grown garlic, chamomile, and other herbal medicines in their gardens. Today, you can buy them in health-food stores. You can get them in dried, powdered, or pill form.

3 After you read

A Check your understanding.

1. What is the reading about?
2. What is the word for the sections of the garlic bulb?
3. What do people use garlic for?
4. What does the chamomile plant look like?
5. What can you make from chamomile?
6. What do people use chamomile for?
7. Which plant could you use for high blood pressure?

B Build your vocabulary.

1. Read the dictionary entry for *digestion*. What part of speech is it? What does it mean? What is the antonym? What is the verb? What is the adjective?

> **digestion** /n/ the ability of the body to change food so the body can use it; antonym: **indigestion**; **digest** /v/ – **digestive** /adj/

2. Use a dictionary. Fill in the chart with the missing forms.

Noun	Verb	Adjective
digestion	*digest*	*digestive*
	prevent	
sickness		
	treat	
herbs		

3. Complete the sentences. Write the correct form of the word from Exercise B2.
   a. You shouldn't swim right after you eat. You should wait to ___*digest*___ your food.
   b. Chamomile, basil, oregano, and thyme are examples of _____.
   c. Some people can't drink milk. It makes them _____.
   d. Some people drink orange juice to _____ a cold or the flu. They don't want to get sick.
   e. A hot bath is a good _____ for sore muscles.

C Talk with a partner. Ask and answer the questions.

1. How can you prevent a sore throat? A cold? Weight gain?
2. In your opinion, what is the best treatment for a headache? A stomachache? An earache?
3. What herbs do you like to cook with? What's your favorite herb?

☑ Identify the topic of a text by reading the first and last paragraphs; recognize word families

LESSON E Writing

1 Before you write

A **Talk** with a partner. Answer the questions.

1. Do you or your family members ever use beneficial plants?
2. Which ones do you use?
3. What do you use them for?

Aloe vera

B **Read** the paragraph.

Licorice

    Licorice is a popular herb in my native country, Greece. The plant has feathery leaves and purple flowers. It tastes sweet. My mother used to use licorice to make a medicine for my grandmother's arthritis. Mother grew the licorice plant in our backyard. She used to cut the licorice roots into pieces and put them inside a warm, wet cloth. Then she put the cloth on my grandmother's shoulders and knees. The licorice helped with the pain. Today, I use licorice when I have sore muscles.

Work with a partner. Put the information from the paragraph in order.

____ how the writer's mother used the plant

_1_ where the plant grows

____ how the plant helped

____ how the plant tastes

____ how the plant looks

____ how the writer uses the plant today

> The first sentence of a paragraph is called the *topic sentence*. It names the topic and gives basic information about it.
>
> *Licorice* (topic) *is a popular herb in my native country, Greece.* (basic information)

C **Write** a plan for a paragraph about a beneficial plant. Answer the questions.

What's the name of the beneficial plant?	
What do people use it for?	
Where does the plant grow?	
What does the plant look like?	
Can you eat the plant? What does it taste like?	
What does the plant smell like?	
What does the plant feel like?	

2 Write

Write a paragraph about a plant that people use as medicine. Name the herb and give basic information about it in the topic sentence. Describe the plant and how people use it. Use Exercises 1B and 1C to help you.

3 After you write

A **Check** your writing.

	Yes	No
1. In my topic sentence, I named the plant and gave basic information about it.	☐	☐
2. I described the plant.	☐	☐
3. I explained how people use the plant.	☐	☐

B **Share** your writing with a partner.

1. Take turns. Read your paragraph to a partner.
2. Comment on your partner's paragraph. Ask your partner a question about the paragraph. Tell your partner one thing you learned.

LESSON F Another view

Medical History Form

1. Chief complaint: Describe the problem and approximately when it began.

Problem	Date problem began

2. Have you ever had any of the following?

☐ allergies	☐ back pain	☐ frequent headaches	☐ high blood pressure
☐ arthritis	☐ chest pains	☐ heart attack	☐ high cholesterol
☐ asthma	☐ diabetes	☐ heart disease	☐ tuberculosis

3. Are you pregnant? Yes No

4. Are you currently taking medications? Yes No

5. If yes, list all medications, including vitamins and herbal supplements.

_____

6. List any major illness, injury, or surgery that you have had in the past year.

_____

The above information is correct to the best of my knowledge.

7. Signature: _____   **8.** Date: _____

A **Read** the questions. Look at the form. Fill in the answer.

1. Where do you write the reason for this doctor visit?

  Ⓐ number 1 Ⓒ number 4

  Ⓑ number 3 Ⓓ number 5

2. Where do you write the names of the medicines you take?

  Ⓐ number 2 Ⓒ number 5

  Ⓑ number 4 Ⓓ number 7

3. Where do you write that you had back surgery last year?

  Ⓐ number 1 Ⓒ number 5

  Ⓑ number 2 Ⓓ number 6

4. Where do you write when the problem began?

  Ⓐ number 1 Ⓒ number 5

  Ⓑ number 3 Ⓓ number 6

B **Work** with a partner. First, complete the form about yourself or someone you know. Then ask questions about your partner's form. Are the medical histories similar?

2 **Grammar connections:** reported *commands*

Commands	Reported commands
"**Park** over there."	The policewoman **told me to park** over there.
"**Don't talk** during tests."	The teacher **told us not to talk** during tests.

A **Work** with a partner. Complete the chart with commands the people might give.

	Commands	Reported commands
A teacher	Affirmative: *"Listen carefully ."*	Affirmative: *He told us to listen carefully.*
	Negative: *"Don't ."*	Negative: _____.
A police officer	Affirmative: " _____."	Affirmative: _____.
	Negative: " _____."	Negative: _____.

B **Talk** with a partner. Use a reported command to say what a person in the list below might say. Your partner guesses who said it. Take turns.

a dentist	an eye doctor	a parent	a soccer coach
a doctor	a manager	a police officer	a teacher

> **A** This person told me to wear my glasses every day.
> **B** An eye doctor!
> **A** Yes! That's right!

3 **Wrap up**

Complete **the Self-assessment** on page 137.

Review

1 Listening

CLASS CD1 TK 30

Listen. Put a check (✓) under the correct name(s).

	Jenny	Sara
1. used to have time to call friends	✓	
2. used to work 50 hours a week		
3. used to exercise more		
4. used to cook healthy food		
5. used to take care of herself		
6. used to take the stairs at work		

Talk with a partner. Check your answers.

2 Grammar

A Write. Complete the story. Use the correct words.

A Happy Ending

Last year, Frank went to his doctor _____because of_____ his health. His doctor

                                                           1. because / because of

told him that his blood pressure was _____ high. Frank got very

                                                      2. enough / too

nervous because he didn't _____ have health problems.

                                     3. use to / used to

    Frank _____ to get in shape lately. He _____ take the

        4. started / has started   5. use to / used to

elevator at work, but now he takes the stairs. He _____ a lot more

                                            6. has / has had

energy lately. The hardest thing he _____ recently is his favorite

                                      7. has given up / gives up

food – ice cream!

B Write. Look at the answers. Write the questions.

1. **A** _____ Frank _____ lately?

   B Yes, he has. Frank has started to get in shape.

2. **A** _____ Frank _____?

   B Yes, he did. Frank went to the doctor last year because of his health.

3. **A** _____ Frank _____?

   B Yes, he did. Frank used to take the elevator at work.

Talk with a partner. Ask and answer the questions.

3 Pronunciation: voiced and voiceless *th* sounds

CLASS CD1 TK 31

A **Listen** to the *th* sounds in these phrases.

1. **th**is morning	5. **th**e neighbors	9. asked **th**em
2. sore **th**roat	6. on South Street	10. **th**ree times
3. **Th**at's too bad!	7. **th**ey are	11. How are **th**ings?
4. heal**th** problems	8. **th**is month	12. **th**anks

Listen again and repeat.

CLASS CD1 TK 32

B **Listen and repeat.** Then underline the words with the voiced and voiceless *th* sounds.

1. A Where's Tommy <u>this</u> morning?
   B He's sick. He has a sore throat.
   A That's too bad!
   B He often has health problems.
   A I'm sorry to hear that.

2. A The neighbors on South Street are really noisy.
   B Yes, they are.
   A This month, I've asked them three times to be quiet.
   B Let's write them a letter.
   A That's a good idea.

Talk with a partner. Compare your answers.

C **Talk** with a partner. Practice the conversations. Pay attention to the words with the *th* sounds.

1. A What can your friends do to be more healthy?
   B Well, they can exercise more this month.
   A That's a good idea.
   B And they can eat healthy meals three times a day.

2. A How are things?
   B Not great. I have three tests this week.
   A Oh, I think you'll do fine.
   B Thanks.

D **Write** four questions. Use the words in Exercise 3A. Ask your partner.

Have you eaten this morning?

1. _____
2. _____
3. _____
4. _____

UNIT 5 Around town

LESSON A
Listening

1 Before you listen

A What do you see?

B What is happening?

C What's the story?

2 Listen

STUDENT TK 19
CLASS CD1 TK 33

A Listen and answer the questions.

1. Who are the speakers?
2. What are they talking about?

STUDENT TK 19
CLASS CD1 TK 33

B Listen again. Read and match the events. You may use an event more than once.

1. It opens at 10:00. __c__
2. It starts at 10:30. __d__
3. It starts at 11:00. __b__
4. The family will do this first. __c__
5. The family will do this if the weather is nice. __a__

a. outdoor concert
b. garden tour
c. art exhibit
d. storytelling

3 After you listen

A Read. Complete the story.

admission	concert	exhibit	storytelling
afford	events	options	tour

It is Thursday. Wen and Mei are talking about their plans for the weekend.

They can't ___afford___ to spend a lot of money on entertainment. They decide
                      1

to check the newspaper for free community ___events___ on Sunday. They have
                                              2

many ___options___. There's an outdoor ___concert___ in the park, a walking
          3   4

___tour___ of the gardens, a modern art ___exhibit___ at the art museum, and
    5   6

storytelling for children at the library. All these events have free ___admission___
                                                                         7

The problem is that all these things are happening on Sunday at the same time.

Mei and Wen decide to take their son to the ___storytelling___ first. Then, if the weather
                                                 8

is nice, they will go to the concert. Later, they might go to the art museum.

STUDENT TK 20
CLASS CD1 TK 34

Listen and check your answers.

B Talk with a partner. Ask and answer the question.

What kind of entertainment do you enjoy on the weekend?

LESSON B Verbs + infinitives

1 Grammar focus: questions and answers

Questions	Answers

Where do you **plan to go**?

I **plan to go** to the park.

Do you **plan to go** to the park?

Yes, I do. | No, I don't.

infinitive =
to + base form of verb

Verbs infinitives often follow

agree	decide	hope	need	promise	want
(can / can't) afford	expect	intend	plan	refuse	would like

Turn to page 142 for a complete grammar chart and explanation.

2 Practice

A Write. Complete the sentences.

1. A How much do you ___expect to pay___ for the concert?
   (expect / pay)
   B No more than $25.

2. A What have you _decided to do_ for your birthday?
   (decided / do)
   B I'm going to an exhibit at the art museum.

3. A Can you _afford to buy_ a ticket for the show?
   (afford / buy)
   B Not really. I need to start saving money.

   > **USEFUL** LANGUAGE
   >
   > *afford to do something =
   > have enough money to do it*

4. A What did you _agree to do_ next weekend?
   (agree / do)
   B We agreed to go to the park.

5. A How does Tom _intend to get_ to the park?
   (intend / get)
   B He's going to ride his bike.

6. A Have you ever _refused to go_ on a trip with your family?
   (refused / go)
   B No, I haven't.

7. A Did they _promise to visit_ their relatives this weekend?
   (promise / visit)
   B Yes, they did.

 Listen and check your answers. Then practice with a partner.

CLASS CD1 TK 35

B **Talk** with a partner. Ask and answer questions about Sharon's plans. Look at her calendar. Use the verbs in the box and an infinitive.

> **A** What does Sharon plan to do on Tuesday?
> **B** She plans to go to a concert with Linda.

expect   hope   intend   need   plan   want

May

Sunday	Monday	Tuesday	Wednesday	Thursday	Friday	Saturday
		1	2	3	4	5
		12:30 p.m. Go with Linda to a concert.	5:30 p.m. Meet Joe at the gym.	9:00 a.m. See the dentist. 3:00 p.m. See the new art exhibit.	7:30 a.m. Go to work with John. 6:00 p.m. Have dinner with Andrew???	Sit on the beach all day!

Write sentences about Sharon's plans.

On Tuesday, Sharon plans to go to a concert with Linda.

3 Communicate

A **Work** in a small group. Choose one item from each column. Answer questions about your plans.

> **A** What do you expect to do tomorrow?
> **B** I plan to meet my friends for lunch tomorrow.

expect		tomorrow
hope		next week
intend		next month
need	(infinitive of any verb)	next year
plan		two years from now
want		three years from now
would like		five years from now

B **Share** information about your classmates.

☑ **Use verbs + infinitives** **UNIT 5** **61**

LESSON C Present perfect

1 Grammar focus: *already* and *yet*

Yes/No questions

Have you **bought** the tickets **yet**?
Has she **already** seen the movie?

Short answers

Yes, I **have**.	No, I **haven't**.
Yes, she **has**.	No, she **hasn't**.

Affirmative statements

I've **already** bought the tickets.
She's **already** seen the movie.

Negative statements

I **haven't** bought the tickets **yet**.
She **hasn't** seen the movie **yet**.

Past participles: Irregular verbs

begin → begun	get → gotten	put → put
bring → brought	go → gone	read → read
buy → bought	make → made	set → set
do → done	pay → paid	

Turn to page 143 for a complete grammar chart and explanation.
Turn to page 146 for a list of irregular verbs.

2 Practice

A Write. Complete the sentences. Use *already* or *yet*.

1. It's 11:00 p.m. The salsa concert has ___*already*___ ended.

2. It's 8:00 a.m. The science museum opens at 9:00. It hasn't opened _____.

3. It's July 5th. The Independence Day parade has _____ finished.

4. It's the beginning of August. School begins in September. School activities haven't begun _____.

5. It's 2:00 a.m. The dance club stays open until 3:00. It hasn't closed _____.

6. It's Friday evening. The weekend has _____ started.

7. It's 7:45 p.m. The movie starts at 8:00. We haven't missed the movie _____.

8. It's Monday. I've _____ bought tickets for next Sunday's soccer game.

Listen and check your answers.

CLASS CD1 TK 36

B **Talk** with a partner. Jaime and Andrea are helping at their school's fund-raiser. Ask and answer questions about them. Use *yet*.

> **A** Has Jaime bought refreshments yet?
> **B** Yes, he has.
> **A** Has Andrea set up the tables yet?
> **B** No, she hasn't.

> **CULTURE** NOTE
>
> A *fund-raiser* is an event where people collect money for a school, an organization, or a cultural activity.

Things to do before the fund-raiser

Jaime

- ✓ buy refreshments
- ✓ borrow more chairs
- call the chair-rental store
- get name tags
- pick up the DJ

Andrea

- set up the tables
- ✓ organize the volunteers
- ✓ make the food
- bring the music CDs
- ✓ put up the decorations

Write sentences about Jaime and Andrea. Use *already* and *yet*.

Jaime has already bought refreshments.

Andrea hasn't set up the tables yet.

3 Communicate

A **Work** with a partner. Ask and answer questions. Complete the chart.

> **A** Have you done your homework yet?
> **B** Yes, I have.
> **A** Have you already paid your bills?
> **B** No, I haven't.

Activities	Yes	No
1. do your homework	☐	☐
2. pay your bills	☐	☐
3. go to a baseball game in this country	☐	☐
4. read the newspaper today	☐	☐
5. (your question)	☐	☐
6. (your question)	☐	☐

B **Share** information about your classmates.

☑ Use present perfect with *already* and *yet*   **UNIT 5**   **63**

LESSON **D** Reading

1 Before you read

Talk with your classmates. Answer the questions.

1. Do you like salsa music?
2. Have you ever gone to an outdoor concert? Where? When?

2 Read

STUDENT TK 21
CLASS CD1 TK 37

Read the concert review. Listen and read again.

> When you see a new word, try to guess if the meaning is positive or negative.
> *The volume was **excessive**.*
> *I had to wear my earplugs.*
> You can guess that *excessive* has a negative meaning.

Salsa Starz
at Century Park

If you missed the outdoor concert at Century Park last Saturday evening, you missed a great night of salsa music and dancing – and the admission was free!

The performers were the popular band Salsa Starz. Bandleader Ernesto Sanchez led the five-piece group and two dancers. Sanchez is a versatile musician.

He sang and played maracas and guitar. The other musicians were also superb. The group's excellent playing and great energy galvanized the crowd. No one sat down during the entire show!

However, the evening had some problems. At first, the sound level of the music was excessive. I had to wear earplugs.

Then, the level was too low. The change in sound was irritating. In addition, the stage was plain and unremarkable. I expected to see lights and lots of color at the performance. The weather was another problem. The night started out clear. By 10:00 p.m., some ominous black clouds moved in, and soon it started to rain. The band intended to play until 11:00, but the show ended early because of the rain.

Century Park has free concerts every Saturday evening in July and August. If you haven't attended one of these concerts yet, plan to go next weekend. But take an umbrella!

3 After you read

A Check your understanding.

1. Where did Salsa Starz perform?
2. What were two positive things about the concert?
3. What were three negative things?
4. Did the audience like the concert? How do you know?
5. How do you think the reviewer rated the overall performance? Find the words in the reading to support your opinion.

**** excellent   *** very good   ** OK   * bad

B Build your vocabulary.

1. Find these words in the reading, and underline them. Which words are positive? Which words are negative? What clues helped you guess?

Word	Positive	Negative	Clue
1. versatile	✓	☐	*He sang and played maracas and guitar.*
2. superb	☐	☐	
3. galvanized	☐	☐	
4. excessive	☐	☐	
5. irritating	☐	☐	
6. unremarkable	☐	☐	
7. ominous	☐	☐	

2. Work with your classmates. Write four more words in the reading that have a positive or negative meaning. Write *P* next to positive words. Write *N* next to negative words.

a. _____   c. _____

b. _____   d. _____

C Talk with a partner.

1. Tell your partner about a superb restaurant.
2. Tell about a versatile artist.
3. Tell about an irritating experience.
4. Tell about an unremarkable TV program.

LESSON E Writing

1 Before you write

A **Talk** with your classmates.

1. Do you use e-mail? How often?
2. What do you use it for?

B **Read** the e-mail.

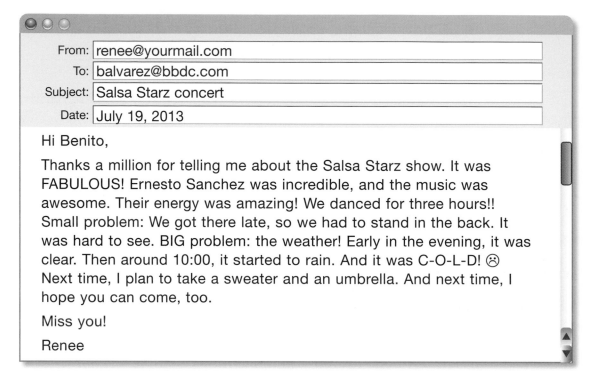

From: renee@yourmail.com

To: balvarez@bbdc.com

Subject: Salsa Starz concert

Date: July 19, 2013

Hi Benito,

Thanks a million for telling me about the Salsa Starz show. It was FABULOUS! Ernesto Sanchez was incredible, and the music was awesome. Their energy was amazing! We danced for three hours!! Small problem: We got there late, so we had to stand in the back. It was hard to see. BIG problem: the weather! Early in the evening, it was clear. Then around 10:00, it started to rain. And it was C-O-L-D! ☹ Next time, I plan to take a sweater and an umbrella. And next time, I hope you can come, too.

Miss you!

Renee

Work with a partner. Complete the diagram with positive and negative information about the concert.

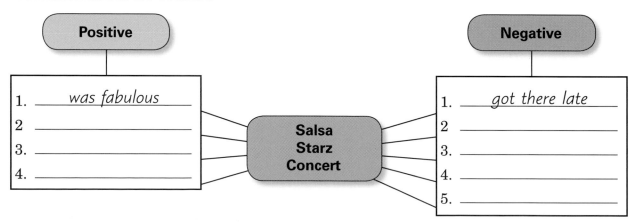

Positive

1. _was fabulous_
2. _____
3. _____
4. _____

Salsa Starz Concert

Negative

1. _got there late_
2. _____
3. _____
4. _____
5. _____

C **Write** the name of a concert, a movie, or a performance you have seen in the middle of the diagram. Complete the diagram with positive and negative information.

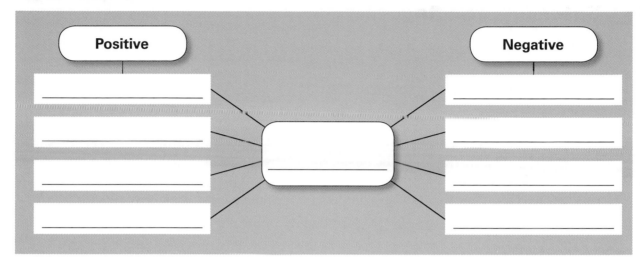

Positive | Negative

Share your information with a partner.

2 Write

Write an e-mail about a concert, a movie, or a performance you have seen. Name the event in your first sentence. Use positive and negative words to describe the event. Use an informal writing style in the e-mail. Use Exercises 1B and 1C to help you.

The style of a friendly e-mail is informal.
- Some sentences are not complete.
  Miss you!
  BIG problem: the weather!
- Writers use capital letters and symbols to express their feelings.
  It was FABULOUS!
  It was C-O-L-D! ☹

3 After you write

A **Check** your writing.

	Yes	No
1. I named the event in my first sentence.	☐	☐
2. I used positive and negative words to describe the event.	☐	☐
3. I used an informal writing style in my e-mail.	☐	☐

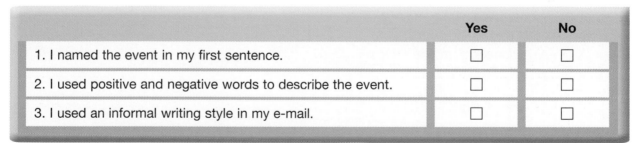

B **Share** your writing with a partner.

1. Take turns. Read your e-mail to a partner.
2. Comment on your partner's e-mail. Ask your partner a question about the e-mail. Tell your partner one thing you learned.

LESSON F Another view

1 Life-skills reading

Announcements

Travel Movies
Join us at 7:00 p.m. on Saturday and
Sunday to see movies on India, Japan, and
Brazil. Kids welcome. Downtown Public
Library. Come early – seating is limited.

Concerts on the Green
Hear the Riverside Brass Band every
Friday this month at noon. North end of
City Park, near the courthouse.

Crafts Fair
Find gifts for your family and friends.
Jewelry, pottery, paintings, and food from
around the world. Sunday from 9:00 a.m.
to 5:00 p.m. at Broadway and 5th Street.

Fix a Flat
Bike Master Shop offers basic bicycle
maintenance clinics this Saturday at
4:30 p.m. and Sunday at 9:00 a.m. in front
of the Bike Master Shop.

A Read the questions. Look at the announcements. Fill in the answer.

1. At which event can you buy food?
   - (A) Concerts on the Green
   - (B) Crafts Fair
   - (C) Travel Movies
   - (D) all of the above

2. Which event does not happen during the day?
   - (A) Concerts on the Green
   - (B) Crafts Fair
   - (C) Fix a Flat
   - (D) Travel Movies

3. Which event would be good for bike riders?
   - (A) Crafts Fair
   - (B) Fix a Flat
   - (C) Travel Movies
   - (D) none of the above

4. Which event is at noon on Saturday?
   - (A) Concerts on the Green
   - (B) Fix a Flat
   - (C) Travel Movies
   - (D) none of the above

B Talk with a partner. Ask and answer the questions.

1. Which activity would you like to attend? Why?
2. What other activities or events do you like to attend?

2 Grammar connections: verbs + infinitives and verbs + gerunds

Verbs + infinitives	Verbs + gerunds	Verbs + infinitives or gerunds
decide need refuse intend plan want	avoid enjoy miss dislike finish suggest	continue like start hate prefer
We **intend to study** tonight. We **need to go** home.	Tomas **dislikes exercising**. They **enjoy swimming**.	I **like to cook**. I **like cooking**.

A **Work** in a small group. Ask the questions with *to do* or *doing*. Complete the survey.

A What do you enjoy doing on
the weekend, Viktor?
B I enjoy walking in the park.
A What do you intend to do
after class?
B I intend to study at the library.

What do you . . .	(name)	(name)	(name)
enjoy _____ on the weekend?			
intend _____ after class?			
avoid _____ at home?			
hate _____ in the morning?			
refuse _____ on the weekend?			
plan _____ at the end of the year?			
like _____ in the summer?			
miss _____ from your childhood?			

B **Share** information about your classmates.

*Viktor enjoys walking in the park. He intends
to study at the library after class. He . . .*

3 Wrap up

Complete the **Self-assessment** on page 138.

LESSON **A**
Listening

1 **Before you listen**

A What do you see?

B What is happening?

C What's the story?

1.

Winston

2.

3.

To do
1. trash
2.
3.
4.
5.

4.

Unit Goals

Identify tips for time management

Explain U.S. rules about time

Describe qualities and habits of good and weak time managers

2 Listen

STUDENT TK 22
CLASS CD2 TK 2

A **Listen** and answer the questions.

1. Who are the speakers?
2. What are they talking about?

STUDENT TK 22
CLASS CD2 TK 2

B **Listen again.** Complete Winston's to-do list. Then number the tasks in order of priority.

Things to Do	Priority
• take out the trash	1
•	
•	
•	
•	

3 After you listen

A **Read.** Complete the story.

chores   deadline   due   impatient   prioritize   procrastinating   tasks

Winston is listening to music in his room. His mother comes in and tells him to stop _procrastinating_ . She is very _____ because he isn't taking out the
1   2
trash, and he isn't doing his homework.

Winston has too many things to do. His mother suggests making a to-do list. First, she tells him to list all the tasks he needs to do. Next, she tells him to _____
3
– to put his _____ in order of importance. His mother says he needs to do his
4
homework and _____ first. He decides to do his English and math homework
5
first because they are _____ the next day. He also has a history project, but
6
the _____ is next Tuesday. After he finishes his homework, he will practice
7
guitar. But before he does anything else, he has to take out the trash.

STUDENT TK 23
CLASS CD2 TK 3

Listen and check your answers.

B **Talk** with a partner. Ask and answer the question.

When you have a lot of things to do, how do you decide what to do first?

LESSON **B** Adverb clauses

1 Grammar focus: clauses with *when*

When I **have** a lot to do, I **make** a to-do list.

When she **feels** tired, she **takes** a break.

I **make** a to-do list **when** I **have** a lot to do.

She **takes** a break **when** she **feels** tired.

Turn to page 148 for a grammar explanation.

Turn to page 148 for a grammar explanation.

USEFUL LANGUAGE

Use a comma when the adverb clause is at the beginning of the sentence. When you read out loud, pause after the comma.

2 Practice

A **Write.** Combine the sentences. Use *when*. Circle the adverb clause.

Tips for Managing Your Time

1. You have many things to do. Make a to-do list.

   When (__*you have many things to do*__), __*make a to-do list*__.

2. You have a deadline. Write it on your calendar.

   When _____, _____.

3. Don't let people interrupt you. You need to concentrate.

   _____ when _____.

4. You want to focus on a task. Turn off the television.

   When _____, _____.

5. You feel tired. Take a break.

   When _____, _____.

6. Give yourself a reward. You finish something difficult.

   _____ when _____.

7. Don't procrastinate. You have a deadline.

   _____ when _____.

8. You are tired. Don't do difficult tasks.

   When _____, _____.

Listen and check your answers.

CLASS CD2 TK 4

B **Talk** with a partner. Make sentences with *when*.

> **A** When Mr. Jackson has a deadline, **he doesn't answer** the phone.
> **B** Ms. Clark **answers every call** when she has a deadline.

Mr. Jackson

Ms. Clark

1. doesn't answer the phone	answers every call
2. closes his office door	allows people to interrupt
3. does one task at a time	does several things at once
4. does difficult tasks first	procrastinates

Write sentences about Mr. Jackson and Ms. Clark.

Mr. Jackson doesn't answer the phone when he has a deadline.

3 Communicate

A **Work** in a small group. Interview your classmates. Complete the chart.

> **A** What do you do when you have a deadline?
> **B** I usually procrastinate.
> **C** I start working right away.

What do you do when you . . .	Name: _____	Name: _____	Name: _____
have a deadline?	*procrastinate*		
have many things to do?			
finish a difficult task?			
have trouble concentrating?			
(your idea)			

B **Share** information about your classmates.

LESSON C Adverb clauses

1 Grammar focus: clauses with *before* and *after*

Before she **eats** breakfast, she **reads** the newspaper.

After I **watch** the news, I **eat** dinner.

She **reads** the newspaper **before** she **eats** breakfast.

I **eat** dinner **after** I **watch** the news.

Turn to page 148 for a grammar explanation.

USEFUL LANGUAGE

Use a comma when *before* and *after* clauses are at the beginning of a sentence. When you read out loud, pause after the comma.

2 Practice

A Read Bonnie's morning schedule. Write sentences with *before* and *after*.

Bonnie's Morning Schedule

6:55 take a shower	7:35 bring in the newspaper
7:15 get dressed	7:40 eat breakfast
7:30 make coffee	8:00 leave for work

take a shower / get dressed

1. After _Bonnie takes a shower_ , _she gets dressed_ .
2. _Bonnie takes a shower_ before _she gets dressed_ .

get dressed / make coffee

3. Before _____ , _____ .
4. _____ after _____ .

bring in the newspaper / eat breakfast

5. _____ before _____ .
6. _____ after _____ .

eat breakfast / leave for work

7. After _____ , _____ .
8. Before _____ , _____ .

 Listen and check your answers.

B Talk with a partner. Ask and answer questions about Ken, a soap opera star. Use *before* and *after*.

A What does Ken do before he goes to the studio? **B** Before Ken goes to the studio, he works out.	**A** What does Ken do after he works out? **B** Ken goes to the studio after he works out.

1. works out 2. goes to the studio 3. memorizes his lines

4. puts on makeup 5. performs his scene 6. goes home and rests

Write sentences about Ken's day.

Ken works out before he goes to the studio.

3 Communicate

A Work in a small group. Ask and answer questions about daily activities. Complete the chart.

A What do you do every day, Emma? **B** I study. **A** What do you do before you study? **B** I watch TV.	**A** What do you do after you study? **B** I go to bed.

Name	Everyday activity	Before activity	After activity
Emma	study	watch TV	go to bed

B Share information about your classmates.

LESSON **D** Reading

1 Before you read

Look at the title. Answer the questions.

1. What are some rules about time in this country?
2. What are some rules about time in other countries?

2 Read

Read this article. Listen and read again.

STUDENT TK 24
CLASS CD2 TK 6

RULES about TIME

Every culture has rules about time. These rules are usually unspoken, but everybody knows them.

In some countries such as the United States, England, and Canada, punctuality is an unspoken rule. It is important to be on time, especially in business. People usually arrive a little early for business appointments. Business meetings and personal appointments often have strict beginning and ending times. When you are late, other people might think you are rude, disorganized, or irresponsible.

These countries also have cultural rules about time in social situations. For example, when an invitation for dinner says 6:00 p.m., it is impolite to arrive more than five or ten minutes late. On the other hand, when the invitation is for a party from 6:00 to 8:00 or a reception from 3:30 to 5:30, you can arrive anytime between those hours. For public events with specific starting times – movies, concerts, sports events – you should arrive a few minutes before the event begins. In fact, some theaters do not allow people to enter if they arrive after the event has started.

Other cultures have different rules about time. In Brazil, it is not unusual for guests to arrive an hour or two after a social event begins. In the Philippines, it is not uncommon for people to miss scheduled events – a class or an appointment – to meet a friend at the airport. Many Filipinos believe that relationships with people are more important than keeping a schedule.

> **Dashes often signal a definition, explanation, or example. The dashes in this reading signal examples.**

3 After you read

A Check your understanding.

1. What are "unspoken" rules?

2. How is your definition of "on time" the same or different from the author's description of the unspoken rules about time in the United States, England, and Canada?

3. What are examples of public events with specific starting times?

4. When should you arrive for the following events in the U.S.? When should you arrive for these same events in your native country?
   - a medical appointment
   - a business meeting
   - dinner at someone's house
   - a party
   - a sports event

B Build your vocabulary.

1. English has several prefixes that mean "not." Write words from the reading that begin with these prefixes.

   un- _____unspoken_____

   dis- _____

   ir- _____

   im- _____

2. Work with a partner. Explain the meaning of the words you wrote.

3. Work with a partner. Write more words with the prefixes. Use a dictionary if needed. Use each word in a sentence.

un-	dis-	ir-	im-

C Talk with a partner. Ask and answer the questions.

1. Your friend is disorganized. What advice can you give your friend?

2. Someone is late to a job interview. Is that person irresponsible? Why or why not?

3. You are 30 minutes late for lunch with a friend. Is it impolite? Why or why not?

LESSON E Writing

1 Before you write

A **Work** in a small group. Discuss the questions. Complete the diagrams.

1. What qualities and habits does a good time manager have?

makes a to-do list

**Good
time manager**

2. What qualities and habits does a weak time manager have?

procrastinates

**Weak
time manager**

B **Talk** with a partner. Answer the questions.

1. What qualities and habits from each diagram do you have?
2. In general, are you a good time manager or a weak time manager? Why do you think so?

C Read the paragraph.

How Lucinda Manages Her Time

Lucinda is not a very good time manager. For example, this is the way she does her homework. First, she sits down and takes out her books. Two minutes later, she decides to get a cup of coffee. She goes to the kitchen, makes coffee, and returns to her desk. Before she starts reading, she checks her e-mail. Then the phone rings. It's her best friend. They talk for 20 minutes. After they hang up, it's 9:00 p.m. – time for Lucinda's favorite TV show. She watches the show from 9:00 to 10:00. Then, she studies from 10:00 until 1:30 a.m. Of course, she is tired in the morning. In summary, Lucinda is a weak time manager because she procrastinates.

> Use one of the following phrases before your conclusion:
> *In conclusion,*
> *To conclude,*
> *In summary,*

Work with a partner. Answer the questions.

1. What is the topic sentence?
2. How many examples does the writer give about Lucinda?
3. Which phrase signals the conclusion?

2 Write

Write a paragraph about yourself or someone you know who is a good or a weak time manager. Say what kind of time manager you are writing about in the topic sentence. Include examples to support your topic sentence and a signal before your conclusion. Use Exercises 1A and 1C to help you.

3 After you write

A Check your writing.

	Yes	No
1. My topic sentence says what kind of time manager I am writing about.	☐	☐
2. I included examples to support my topic sentence.	☐	☐
3. I used a signal before my conclusion.	☐	☐

B Share your writing with a partner.

1. Take turns. Read your paragraph to a partner.
2. Comment on your partner's paragraph. Ask your partner a question about the paragraph. Tell your partner one thing you learned.

LESSON **F** Another view

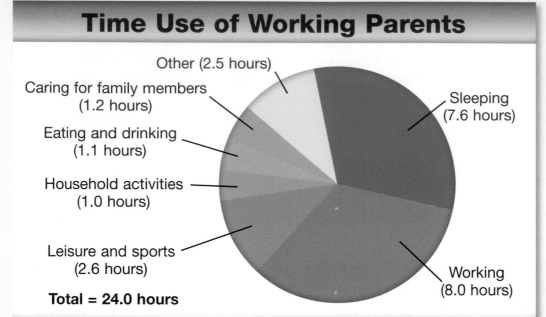

Time Use of Working Parents

Other (2.5 hours)

Caring for family members
(1.2 hours)

Eating and drinking
(1.1 hours)

Household activities
(1.0 hours)

Leisure and sports
(2.6 hours)

Total = 24.0 hours

Sleeping
(7.6 hours)

Working
(8.0 hours)

Source: U.S. Department
of Labor, Bureau of
Labor Statistics
www.bls.gov/tus/charts/
home.htm

A **Read** the questions. Look at the pie chart. Fill in the answer.

1. Who is the chart about?

  Ⓐ employed people with children

  Ⓑ employed people without
  children

  Ⓒ unemployed people with
  children

  Ⓓ none of the above

2. Which activity do these people
spend the least time doing?

  Ⓐ caring for family members

  Ⓑ eating and drinking

  Ⓒ household activities

  Ⓓ none of the above

3. Which activity do these people spend the
most time doing?

  Ⓐ eating and drinking

  Ⓑ leisure and sports

  Ⓒ working

  Ⓓ none of the above

4. Which statement is true?

  Ⓐ People spend less time working than
  eating, drinking, and sleeping combined.

  Ⓑ People spend more time working than
  eating, drinking, and sleeping combined.

  Ⓒ People spend as much time working as
  eating, drinking, and sleeping combined.

  Ⓓ none of the above

B **Talk** with a partner. Ask and answer the questions.

1. About how much time a day do you spend on the activities listed on the pie chart?

2. On which activities do you spend more time than the pie chart shows?

3. On which activities do you spend less time than the pie chart shows?

2 Grammar connections: *one* / *some* / *any* and *it* / *them*

	Use an indefinite pronoun (*one*, *some*, or *any*) to refer to a noun that is not specific.	Use a definite pronoun (*it* or *them*) to refer to a noun that is specific.
Singular	Do you have <u>a bus schedule</u>? Sure. Here's **one**.	Can I see <u>your bus schedule</u>? Sure. Here **it** is.
Plural	Do you have <u>any bus schedules</u>? Sure. There are **some** over there. No, we don't have **any**.	Can I see <u>those bus schedules</u>? Sure. You can take **them**.

A **Work** with a partner. Complete the sentences with *one*, *it*, *some*, *any*, or *them*.

1. **A** Which gate do the buses to Trenton leave from?

   B Which __*one*__ do you want?

   A The 10:15 bus.

   B Let's see, the 10:15 bus? OK . . . _____ leaves from Gate 12.

2. **A** Do you have _____ bags to check?

   B No. I have two bags, but I'd like to bring _____ on the plane.

   A You're only allowed to bring on one small _____. Those are too big.

3. **A** Do you have _____ school assignments, Winston?

   B Yes, I have _____. There are three.

   A When are you going to work on _____?

   B Well, I've already finished two, and started the other. I'll finish _____ tomorrow.

B **Talk** with your classmates. Ask and answer questions. Use *it*, *them*, *one*, *some*, and *any* in your answers.

Have you seen a movie this week?

Yes, I've seen one. / No, I haven't seen one.

1. see / a movie / this week
2. see / the movie / *The Godfather*
3. read / any newspapers / in English?
4. read / last Sunday's / *New York Times*
5. watch / any cooking shows / on TV
6. watch / the Discovery and History Channels

3 Wrap up

Complete the **Self-assessment** on page 138.

☑ Interpret a pie chart; contrast *one* and *it* with *some*, *any*, and *them* **UNIT 6** **81**

Review

1 Listening

CLASS CD2 TK 7

Listen. Put a check (✓) under the correct name.

	Trina	Minh
1. has decided to visit his family		✓
2. is going to Las Vegas		
3. hasn't bought plane tickets yet		
4. has already made reservations		
5. won a free hotel room		

Talk with a partner. Check your answers.

2 Grammar

A **Write.** Complete the story. Use the correct words.

A Great Time Manager

Natalia Alvarez begins work at 8:00 in the morning. It is 7:50 and she has already

_____*arrived*_____ at her job. She is a single parent, so she needs _____
  1. arrive / arrived   2. manage / to manage

her time well. Every Saturday _____ she goes shopping, she makes a
                                3. before / after

list of all the food she needs. _____ she takes her children to the park on
                                  4. When / After

Sunday, she cooks meals for the rest of the week. When she _____ home
                                                            5. has come / comes

late, she just heats up the food she cooked on Sunday. After she helps her children with

their homework, she _____ the laundry and goes to bed. Natalia is a
                      6. do / does

great time manager.

B **Write.** Look at the answers. Write the questions.

1. **A** What does Natalia do before _____?

   B Natalia makes a list before she goes shopping.

2. **A** What _____?

   B She cooks meals for the rest of the week after she goes to the park.

3. **A** When _____?

   B She does the laundry after she helps her children with their homework.

Talk with a partner. Ask and answer the questions.

3 Pronunciation: initial *st* sound

CLASS CD2 TK 8

A Listen to the initial *st* sound.

1. **St**udy English.
2. **St**art the computer.
3. Tell the **st**ory.
4. What **st**ate do you live in?
5. Go to the **st**ore.
6. **St**udents need to **st**udy.
7. Let's see the Salsa **St**arz.
8. **St**op procrastinating.

Listen again and repeat.

CLASS CD2 TK 9

B Listen and repeat. Then underline the initial *st* sound.

1. **A** Hi, Stuart. I'm going to the store. What do you need?

   B Can you get me some stamps? It's the first of the month, and I have to pay bills.

   A Sure.

   B Thanks. I'll start writing the checks now and stop procrastinating.

2. **A** Hello, Stephanie.

   B Hi, Steve. Are you still a student here?

   A Yes. I'm studying appliance repair.

   B Really? Maybe you can fix my stove when you're finished.

   A I hope so.

Talk with a partner. Compare your answers.

C Talk with a partner. Ask and answer the questions. Say the words with the initial *st* sound carefully.

1. How long have you studied at this school?
2. When you go to the store, what do you usually buy?
3. When did you move to this state?
4. When did you start working?

D Write five questions. Use the following words. Ask your partner the questions. Remember to pay attention to the initial *st* sound.

1. study: _____
2. store: _____
3. start: _____
4. story: _____
5. student: _____

LESSON A
Listening

1 **Before you listen**

A What do you see?

B What is happening?

C What's the story?

Unit Goals | **Identify** spending habits
Read about financial problems and solutions
Give financial advice

UNIT 7

2 Listen

STUDENT TK 25
CLASS CD2 TK 10

A **Listen** and answer the questions.

1 Who are the speakers?

2. What are they talking about?

STUDENT TK 25
CLASS CD2 TK 10

B **Listen again.** Complete the chart.

	How much / many?
1. cost of a new car	$27,500
2. cost of a car with tax and fees	
3. money in the savings account	
4. interest rate (%)	
5. months to pay	
6. cost of a used car	

3 After you listen

A **Read.** Complete the story.

afford   balance   cash   credit   debt   financing   interest   pay off

Ken and his wife, Julie, are looking at cars. Ken wants to buy a new car that costs
over $27,000. Julie thinks that they can't ___*afford*___ to spend that much money.
                                              1
The _____ in their savings account is less than $8,000. She's afraid of getting
          2
into _____. But Ken says they can get _____ to help pay for the new
       3   4
car. The _____ rate is low, and they can take five years to _____ the
            5   6
loan. Ken isn't worried about buying things on _____.
                                                   7

Julie disagrees. She suggests that they could buy a used car. She says her father
never had a credit card. He always paid _____ for everything.
                                            8

STUDENT TK 26
CLASS CD2 TK 11

Listen and check your answers.

B **Talk** with a partner. Ask and answer the questions.

1. What things do people often buy on credit?

2. Is it a good idea to buy things on credit? Why or why not?

USEFUL LANGUAGE

*to buy on credit = to buy
something now and pay
for it later*

☑ Listen for and identify numbers related to a purchase   **UNIT 7**   **85**

LESSON B Modals

1 Grammar focus: *could* and *should*

could for suggestions

| You **could get** a smaller car and save money. |
| He **could keep** his money in a savings account. |

should for advice

| What **should** I do? | You **should open** a savings account. |

Turn to page 145 for a complete grammar chart and explanation.

2 Practice

A Write. Complete the sentences. Use *could* or *should*.

> **USEFUL** LANGUAGE
>
> For suggestions, you can say:
> *Why don't you* + verb . . . ?
> *How about* + noun . . . ?
> *How about* + verb + -*ing* . . . ?

1. **A** My rent is going up again. What should I do?

   B Here's my advice. You're a good tenant. I think you ___should___ talk to your landlord.

2. **A** I have to fix my credit. What should I do?

   B You _____ talk to a debt counselor. He can help you.

3. **A** Can you suggest a nice restaurant? It's my wife's birthday.

   B You _____ try Chao's – or how about Anita's?

4. **A** It's my niece's sixteenth birthday next week. What could I get her?

   B Why don't you get tickets to a concert? Or you _____ buy her a CD.

5. **A** That vocational school is very expensive. I can't afford it. Can you give me any advice?

   B Well, you're a good student. I think you _____ apply for a scholarship.

6. **A** I need a new car. Where do you suggest I look for one?

   B How about looking in the newspaper? Or you _____ look online.

CLASS CD2 TK 12

Listen and check your answers. Then practice with a partner.

B Talk with a partner. Take turns. Read the problems. Make suggestions or give advice.

> **A** My car broke down.
> **B** You could take the bus, or you could ask someone for a ride.

1. "My car broke down."

2. "My rent is going up $150!"

3. "It's getting cold in here."

4. "I can't afford a new washing machine."

5. "These shoes look terrible."

6. "I don't have enough cash to pay for these groceries."

Write a suggestion or advice for each picture.

You could take the bus, or you could ask someone for a ride.

3 Communicate

A Work in a small group. Make suggestions or give advice.

- Helene spends too much money on food.
- Gregory spends too much money on clothes.
- Teresa spends too much money on rent.
- Youssef spends too much money on cell phone calls.

B Share your ideas with your classmates.

LESSON C Gerunds after prepositions

1 Grammar focus: questions and answers

Questions	Answers
What are you **thinking about** doing?	I'm **thinking about buying** a car.
What is she **afraid of**?	She's **afraid of losing** her job.
What are they **interested in** doing?	They're **interested in applying** for a loan.

Phrases gerunds often follow

afraid of	thank (someone) for
excited about	think about
happy about	tired of
interested in	worried about

gerund = base form
of verb + *-ing*

Turn to page 141 for a complete grammar chart and explanation.

2 Practice

A Write. Complete the sentences. Use gerunds.

1. I'm worried about _____*paying*_____ interest on my credit card balance.
    (pay)

2. Rob is afraid of _____ into debt. He pays for everything with cash.
    (get)

3. Have you thought about _____ a checking account?
    (open)

4. Elizabeth is happy about _____ an apartment she can afford.
    (find)

5. Elena is excited about _____ classes at the community college.
    (start)

6. I'm tired of _____ payments on my car.
    (make)

7. Franco isn't interested in _____ for a loan.
    (apply)

8. Thank you for _____ me money for school.
    (lend)

9. We're thinking about _____ a house.
    (buy)

10. They were worried about _____ a loan.
    (get)

Listen and check your answers.

CLASS CD2 TK 13

B **Talk** with a partner. Ask and answer questions.

> **A** What's she happy about?
> **B** She's happy about opening a checking account.

1. happy about / open a checking account

2. thinking about / buy a computer

3. worried about / be in debt

4. interested in / study auto mechanics

5. tired of / wait in line

6. excited about / buy a new car

Write a sentence about each picture.

She's happy about opening a checking account.

3 Communicate

A **Work** in a small group. Ask and answer questions.

afraid of	excited about	happy about	responsible for
bad at	good at	interested in	tired of

> **A** What are you afraid of?
> **B** I'm afraid of spending too much money.

B **Share** information about your classmates.

☑ Use gerunds after prepositions to ask and answer questions   **UNIT 7**   **89**

LESSON **D** Reading

1 Before you read

Look at the reading tip. Skim the magazine article. Answer the questions.

1. What problem did the people have?
2. How did they solve it?

2 Read

Read the magazine article. Listen and read again.

STUDENT TK 27
CLASS CD2 TK 14

> One way to organize information is to give problems and solutions.

A Credit Card NIGHTMARE

Sun Hi and Joseph Kim got their first credit card a week after they got married. At first, they paid off the balance every month.

The couple's problems began after they bought a new house. They bought new furniture, a big-screen television, and two new computers. To pay for everything, they applied for more and more credit. Soon they had six different credit cards, and they were more than $18,000 in debt.

"It was a nightmare!" says Mrs. Kim. "The interest rates were 19 percent to 24 percent. Our minimum payments were over $750 a month. We both got second jobs, but it wasn't enough. I was so worried about paying off the debt, I cried all the time."

Luckily, the Kims found a solution. They met Dolores Delgado, a debt counselor. With her help, they looked at all of their living expenses and made a family budget. They combined their six credit card payments into one monthly payment with a lower interest rate. Now, their monthly budget for all living expenses is $3,400. Together they earn $3,900 a month. That leaves $500 for paying off their debt.

"We've cut up our credit cards," says Mr. Kim. "No more expensive furniture! In five years, we can pay off our debt. Now we know. Credit cards are dangerous!"

3 After you read

A **Check** your understanding.

1. When did Mr. and Mrs. Kim get their first credit card?
2. When did their problems begin?
3. How did they pay for everything?
4. Mrs. Kim says, "It was a nightmare!" What does she mean?
5. Who is Dolores Delgado, and how did she help the Kims?
6. Do you think the Kims will have financial problems in the future? Why or why not?

B **Build** your vocabulary.

1. Find these words in the reading, and underline them.

credit card	family budget	minimum payments
debt counselor	interest rates	

2. Work with a partner. Circle the correct answers.
   1. Look at the words in Exercise B1. They are compound nouns. In each of the two-word combinations, the first word is:

      a. a noun   b. an adjective

   2. Look at the words again. The second word is:

      a. a noun   b. an adjective

3. Match each compound noun with its meaning.

   1. credit card _____
   2. interest rate _____
   3. minimum payment _____
   4. debt counselor _____
   5. family budget _____

   a. a spending plan that a family makes for itself
   b. a small plastic card that allows you to buy something now and pay for it later
   c. the smallest payment you can make each month on a credit card
   d. the rate – percentage – of interest that you must pay each month on a credit card balance
   e. a person who helps you solve financial problems

4. Work with your classmates. Write other *noun + noun* combinations.

   _____ _____ _____

C **Talk** with your classmates. Ask and answer the questions.

1. How many credit cards do you have? What interest rate do you pay?
2. Do you think credit cards are helpful or harmful? Why?
3. Do you think a family budget is important? Why or why not?

LESSON **E** Writing

1 Before you write

A **Talk** with a partner. Look at the picture. What is the problem? What do you suggest?

B **Read** the letter from a newspaper advice column.

THE MONEY MAN

Dear Money Man,

    I recently got a new job in a downtown office. I need to look nice every day. I've never worked in an office before, and I don't have the right clothes. Most of the women wear suits to work. How can I get a new wardrobe without spending my entire salary? Can you give me advice?

Not Clothes Crazy

Work with a partner. Answer the questions.

1. What is the woman's problem?
2. What do you suggest?

C Read the answer from the Money Man.

Dear Not Clothes Crazy,

It's important to look nice at your job, but you don't need to spend all your money on clothes. I have a few suggestions. First, why don't you buy a black suit with a skirt, jacket, and pants? Then wear a different blouse and jewelry every day for a different look. Second, you could shop at thrift stores. They often have excellent used clothes at very cheap prices. Third, how about talking to the other women in your office? They can tell you about good places to shop. Finally, you should make a monthly budget and follow it carefully. Following a budget is the best way to manage your money.

Money Man

> Use words like *first*, *second*, *third*, and *finally* to list your ideas.

Work with a partner. What does the Money Man suggest?

2 Write

Read the letter. Write an answer. Start with the problem and write two or more suggestions. Use Exercises 1A, 1B, and 1C to help you.

Dear Money Man,

My wife and I have three young children. We both work full-time. When we come home from work, we are very tired and don't want to cook. We eat in fast-food restaurants three or four times a week. It's very expensive. Last night, the bill was $44! How can we save money on dinner?

Fast-Food Dad

3 After you write

A Check your writing.

	Yes	No
1. I started with the problem.	☐	☐
2. I wrote two or more suggestions.	☐	☐
3. I used words like *first* and *second* to list my suggestions.	☐	☐

B Share your writing with a partner.

1. Take turns. Read your letter to a partner.
2. Comment on your partner's letter. Ask your partner a question about the letter. Tell your partner one thing you learned.

LESSON F Another view

1 Life-skills reading

 TOWN **BANK**   CHECKING ACCOUNTS

Choose the plan that's right for you!

	Regular Checking	Premium Checking
Monthly Service Fee	$8	$12
Minimum Daily Balance (to waive the monthly service fee)	$1,000	$5,000
Earn Interest	No	Yes
ATM and Bank Card	Free	Free
Free Checks	No	Yes
Free Internet Banking	Yes	Yes
Free Internet Bill Paying	No	Yes
Free Money Orders and Traveler's Checks	No	Yes

A Read the questions. Look at the bank brochure. Fill in the answer.

1. What does the Regular Checking plan offer?

   Ⓐ a free bank card

   Ⓑ free checks

   Ⓒ free money orders

   Ⓓ none of the above

2. What does the Premium Checking plan offer?

   Ⓐ a free ATM card

   Ⓑ free Internet bill paying

   Ⓒ free traveler's checks

   Ⓓ all of the above

3. With Premium Checking, how much do you need in your account to avoid a monthly service fee?

   Ⓐ $0

   Ⓑ $12

   Ⓒ $1,000

   Ⓓ $5,000

4. Which kind of checking account offers free Internet banking?

   Ⓐ Premium Checking

   Ⓑ Regular Checking

   Ⓒ both *a* and *b*

   Ⓓ neither *a* nor *b*

B Talk with your classmates. Ask and answer the questions.

1. Do you have a checking account? Do you pay a monthly fee? What services does your bank offer you?
2. Which of the accounts from Town Bank do you think is better? Why?

2 Grammar connections: collocations with *get* and *take*

Use *get* with adjectives and some nouns.	Use *take* with other nouns.
get dressed	take a bus / a train / a taxi / a plane
get engaged / married / divorced	take notes / a test / a class
get lost / confused	take a break / a nap
get sick / better	take a bath / a shower
get upset / nervous / tired	take a vacation / a trip
get a job / laid off / fired	take pictures / photos

A Talk with a partner. Point to a circle. Your partner asks a question using *get* or *take*. Answer the question. Take turns.

A Do you get sick very often? **B** No, I don't. I hardly ever get sick.	**A** Have you taken a vacation recently? **B** Yes, I have. I took a vacation to Florida last year.

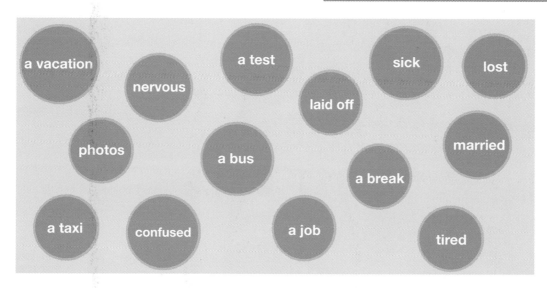

B Share information about your partner.

Manuel doesn't get sick very often.

Anton took a vacation last year. He went to Florida.

3 Wrap up

Complete the **Self-assessment** on page 139.

LESSON A
Listening

1 Before you listen

A What do you see?

B What is happening?

C What's the story?

1. Tony

2. RESUME

3.

4. Human Resources · Mr. Leong · RESUME

2 Listen

A Listen and answer the questions.

STUDENT TK 28
CLASS CD2 TK 15

1. Who are the speakers?

2. What are they talking about?

B Listen again. Complete the chart with information about Tony.

STUDENT TK 28
CLASS CD2 TK 15

Topic	Tony's answers
1. job he is applying for	*shipping-and-receiving clerk*
2. native country	
3. current job	
4. strengths	
5. shift he prefers	

3 After you listen

A Read. Complete the story.

background   degree   employed   gets along   personnel   reliable   strengths

> Tony has been working as a teacher's assistant for about a year. He is also going to college part-time to get a ___*degree*___ in accounting. Right now, Tony is at a job
> 1
> interview with Mr. Leong, the _____ manager.
> 2
>
> Mr. Leong asks about Tony's _____. Tony says he is from Peru and has
> 3
> been living in the United States for two years. Next, Mr. Leong asks about Tony's
> work experience, and Tony says that now he is _____ at a school. Finally,
> 4
> Mr. Leong asks about Tony's personal _____. Tony says he is responsible and
> 5
> _____, and he _____ with everybody. Mr. Leong says he will contact
> 6   7
> Tony next week.

Listen and check your answers.

STUDENT TK 29
CLASS CD2 TK 16

B Talk with a partner. Ask and answer the questions.

Have you ever had a job interview? What happened?

☑ Listen for and identify an applicant's answers to questions in a job interview   **UNIT 8   97**

LESSON B Present perfect continuous

1 Grammar focus: questions and statements

Questions

| Have you **been living** here **for** a long time? |
| Has Tony **been working** here **for** a long time? |

| How long **have** you **been looking** for a job? |
| How long **has** Tony **been working** as a teacher's assistant? |

Short answers

| Yes, I **have**. | No, I **haven't**. |
| Yes, he **has**. | No, he **hasn't**. |

Since October.
For about a year.

Statements

I've **been waiting for** a long time.

Lida **has been waiting since** 2:00.

We've **been waiting all** morning.

Time words
for (a long time)
since (2:00)
all (morning)

USEFUL LANGUAGE

Use *since* with specific times.
Since 2011.
Use *for* with periods of time.
For two months.

Turn to page 144 for a complete grammar chart and explanation.

2 Practice

A Write. Complete the sentences. Use the present perfect continuous.

1. **A** How long _____*has*_____ Talia ___*been practicing*___ for her driving test?
      (practice)
   B For about three months.

2. **A** _____ you _____ here for a long time?
                                      (work)
   B No, I haven't. I started six days ago.

3. **A** How long _____ Yin _____ for a job?
                                                (look)
   B Since last year.

4. **A** _____ Mr. Rivera _____ people all day?
                                             (interview)
   B Yes, he has.

5. **A** How long _____ you _____ to get an interview?
                                              (wait)
   B Since March.

6. **A** How long _____ they _____ to night school?
                                              (go)
   B All year.

 Listen and check your answers. Then practice with a partner.

B **Talk** with a partner. Ask and answer questions.

> **A** How long has Sandra been talking on the phone?
> **B** For 20 minutes.

Sandra

1. talk / for 20 minutes

Ron

2. wait / since 8:00

Latifa

3. study / all morning

Jerry

4. practice keyboarding / since 10:30

Felix and Pablo

5. paint the house / for two days

Sharon

6. work in the restaurant / since 2011

Write a sentence about each picture.

Sandra has been talking on the phone for 20 minutes.

3 Communicate

A **Talk** with your classmates. Find a person who does each activity. Ask how long the person has been doing it. Complete the chart.

> **A** Do you drive?
> **B** Yes, I do.

> **A** How long have you been driving?
> **B** For about six years. / Since 2007.

Activity	Name	How long?
drive	*Josefina*	*for six years / since 2007*
cook for yourself		
attend this school		
work in this country		
play soccer		
use a computer		

B **Share** information about your classmates.

☑ Use present perfect continuous **UNIT 8** **99**

LESSON C Phrasal verbs

1 Grammar focus: separable phrasal verbs

Statements

Alfred **handed out** the papers.
He **handed** the papers **out**.
He **handed** them **out**.

Common separable phrasal verbs

call back	hand out	turn down
clean up	put away	turn off
fill out	throw out / away	turn up

Turn to page 147 for a complete grammar chart and explanation.

Turn to page 147 for a complete grammar chart and explanation.

USEFUL LANGUAGE

papers → them
application → it

2 Practice

A **Write.** Complete the sentences.

1. She's **handing out** papers.
   She's ___handing___ the papers ___out___.
   She's ___handing___ them ___out___.

2. He's _____ the cups.
   He's **throwing** the cups **away**.
   He's _____ them _____.

3. He's _____ the volume.
   He's _____ the volume _____.
   He's **turning** it **up**.

4. She's **filling out** a job application.
   She's _____ the application _____.
   She's _____ it _____.

Listen and check your answers.

CLASS CD2 TK 18

B Talk with a partner. Make requests. Use the verbs in the box.

A Please turn the lights off.
B OK. I'll turn them off.

call back	throw out
clean up	turn down
put away	turn off

1. lights

2. heat

3. lunchroom

4. Mr. Jones

5. trash

6. books

Write sentences about each picture.

Please turn the lights off.

3 Communicate

A Work in a small group. Ask and answer the questions.

1. Have you ever filled out an application form? Where? When?
2. Did you put anything away last night? What was it?
3. Is there someone you need to call back? Who?
4. What things do you want to throw away?
5. What things do you turn on, off, or up?
6. Is there anything you need to clean up? What is it?

B Share information about your classmates.

LESSON D Reading

1 Before you read

Talk with your classmates. Answer the questions.

1. How many dates are in the reading? What are they?
2. What is the reading about?
3. What is a *blog*? Have you ever seen one?

2 Read

 STUDENT TK 30
CLASS CD2 TK 19

Read the blog. Listen and read again.

> Scan the text for specific information. Look quickly to find dates. When you find the information you need, stop reading.

BLOGLAND   <<PREVIOUS BLOG   NEXT BLOG >>   SEARCH

Eden's Blog

Monday 9/29

I had my interview today! I gave the interviewer a big smile and a firm handshake. I answered her questions with confidence. I'll let you know if I get the job.

Thursday 9/25

Great news! One of the companies from the job fair finally called me back! I've been preparing for the job interview all day. I'm really excited. I'm going to have a practice interview with some classmates today. That will prepare me for the real one.

Wednesday 9/24

I've been feeling depressed about the job search lately, but my counselor at school told me I shouldn't give up. He said I need to be patient. Today, I organized my papers. I made lists of the places I have applied to and the people I have talked to. I also did some more research online.

Tuesday 9/16

Today, I went to a job fair at my college. I filled out several applications and handed out some résumés. There were about 20 different companies there. Several of them said they were going to call me back. Wish me luck!

Monday 9/15

Hello fellow job searchers! I have been looking for a job for several weeks. Everyone tells me that it's critical to network, so I've been telling everyone I know. I've been calling friends, relatives, and teachers to tell them about my job search. If you have any good job-searching tips, please share them with me!

3 After you read

A **Scan** the blog for Eden's activities. Match them with the dates.

1. Monday 9/15 _____
2. Tuesday 9/16 _____
3. Wednesday 9/24 _____
4. Thursday 9/25 _____
5. Monday 9/29 _____

a. She had a practice interview with her classmates.
b. She had a job interview.
c. She organized her papers.
d. She's been telling everyone about her job search.
e. She went to a job fair.

B **Check** your understanding.

1. Who wrote the blog?
2. How long has she been looking for a job?
3. Who did she network with?
4. How did she get a job interview?
5. How did she practice for the interview?

> **CULTURE NOTE**
>
> *Blog* comes from the words *Web log*. Readers, or visitors, can visit the Web site and write comments or just read.

C **Build** your vocabulary.

1. Read the dictionary entry for *critical*. How many definitions are there?

> **critical** /adj/ **1** saying that someone or something is bad or wrong **2** giving opinions on books, plays, films, etc. **3** very important; essential – **critically** /adv/

2. Find the vocabulary in the reading. Underline the words. Find each word in a dictionary. Copy the part of speech and the definition that best fits the reading.

Vocabulary	Part of speech	Definition
1. critical	*adjective*	*very important; essential*
2. network		
3. fair		
4. patient		
5. firm		
6. confidence		

D **Talk** with a partner. Ask and answer the questions.

1. What is your most critical goal right now?
2. If you are trying to find a job, who can you network with?
3. How can you show confidence in a job interview?

☑ Scan a blog for steps in a job search; use a dictionary to select the best definition for the context **UNIT 8**

LESSON **E** Writing

1 Before you write

A **Talk** with a partner. Who do you send thank-you letters to? Make a list. Share your list with the class.

B **Read** the thank-you letter.

> 4 South Avenue, Apt. 303
> Kansas City, MO 64115
> September 30, 2013
>
> Janice Hill
> Personnel Manager
> Smart Shop
> 1255 Front Street
> Kansas City, MO 64114
>
> Dear Ms. Hill:
>
> I would like to thank you for the job interview I had with you on Monday, September 29th. I appreciate the time you spent with me. Thank you for showing me around the store and introducing me to some of the employees. I felt very comfortable with them.
>
> Thank you again for your time. I hope to hear from you soon.
>
> Sincerely,
>
> *Eden Babayan*
> Eden Babayan

Work with a partner. Answer the questions.

1. Who wrote the letter?
2. Who did she write it to?
3. What is the writer's address?
4. What is Ms. Hill's address?
5. What information is in the first sentence?
6. How many times did the writer say thank you?
7. How does the writer end the letter?

C **Plan** a formal thank-you letter. Complete the information.

Name and address of the person or business you are thanking:

_____

_____

_____

Reason for saying thank you:

_____

_____

_____

Something specific you appreciate:

_____

_____

_____

2 Write

Write a formal thank-you letter to a person or a business. Say why you are thanking the person and mention something specific that you appreciated. Thank the person again at the end of the letter. Use the letter in Exercise 1B and the information in Exercise 1C to help you.

In a thank-you letter, include:
• why you are thanking the person
• what you appreciate
• another thank you at the end

3 After you write

A **Check** your writing.

	Yes	No
1. My first sentence says why I am thanking the person.	☐	☐
2. I mentioned something specific that I appreciated.	☐	☐
3. I thanked the person again at the end of the letter.	☐	☐

B **Share** your writing with a partner.

1. Take turns. Read your letter to a partner.
2. Comment on your partner's letter. Ask your partner a question about the letter. Tell your partner one thing you learned.

LESSON F Another view

Job Growth for Occupations Requiring an Associate Degree or Vocational Training, 2006 to 2016			
Occupation	Number * of new jobs	Percent increase in growth	Source of postsecondary education
Dental hygienists	50	30.1	Associate Degree
Environmental science and protection technicians, including health	10	28.0	Associate Degree
Makeup artists, theatrical and performance	1	39.8	Postsecondary vocational award
Manicurists and pedicurists	22	27.6	Postsecondary vocational award
Physical therapist assistants	20	32.4	Associate Degree
Skin care specialists	13	34.3	Postsecondary vocational award
Veterinary technologists and technicians	29	41.0	Associate Degree

* Numbers in thousands

Source: http://www.bls.gov/news.release/ooh.t01.htm

A Read the questions. Look at the chart. Fill in the answer.

1. What is not true about the jobs in the chart?
   - (A) They require an associate degree.
   - (B) They require a bachelor degree.
   - (C) They require vocational training.
   - (D) There will be more jobs in 2016 than in 2006.

2. Which occupation will have the largest percent increase in growth from 2006–2016?
   - (A) dental hygienist
   - (B) manicurist
   - (C) physical therapist assistant
   - (D) veterinary technician

3. What is the growth in number of jobs from 2006–2016 for dental hygienists?
   - (A) 50
   - (B) 500
   - (C) 5,000
   - (D) 50,000

4. This chart does not give information about ____ .
   - (A) environmental protection technicians
   - (B) hairdressers
   - (C) pedicurists
   - (D) theatrical artists

B Talk with a partner. Ask and answer the questions.

1. What jobs are growing in your community? Are they the same as the jobs in the chart?
2. Is a job you want on this list?
3. Did anything in this chart surprise you? What was it?

2 Grammar connections: present continuous and present perfect continuous

Use the *present continuous* to talk about an activity that is happening at the moment of speaking.	Use the *present perfect continuous* to talk about an activity that started in the past and continues to the present.
My classmate **is writing** in her book right now.	I've **been writing** e-mails for two hours.

A **Work** in a small group. Play the game. Write your name on a small piece of paper. Flip a coin to move your paper. Then tell your group your answer to the question in the square. Use the present continuous or the present perfect continuous in your answer. Take turns.

= 1 space

= 2 spaces

"Choose someone in the classroom. What is he/she wearing?" OK. I'll describe Tonya. She's wearing . . .

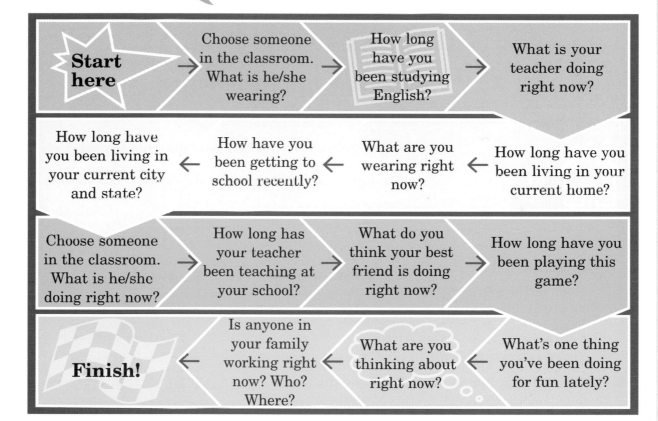

B **Share** information about your classmates.

Tonya is wearing a red and blue sweater.

3 Wrap up

Complete the **Self-assessment** on page 139.

☑ Scan a chart for information; contrast present continuous and present perfect continuous   **UNIT 8**   **107**

Review

1 Listening

Listen. Put a check (✓) under the correct name.

CLASS CD2 TK 20

	Clara	John
1. wants an SUV		✓
2. thinks a small car is better		
3. says an SUV is more comfortable		
4. wants to take friends for a ride		
5. wants to keep taking the bus		
6. wants to save money to buy a house		

Talk with a partner. Check your answers.

2 Grammar

A Write. Complete the story. Use the correct words.

Getting Work Experience

Hao ___*has been applying*___ for jobs as a computer technician since October.
1. will apply / has been applying
He _____ several interviews, but he hasn't gotten a job yet. He's
2. is having / has had
afraid of _____ again until he gets some experience. His friend
3. applying / apply
Terry gave him some good advice. He said Hao _____ think about
4. could / should
_____ at Hao's son's school. Hao wants to call the school because the
5. volunteer / volunteering
school _____ problems with the computer system for a few months.
6. has been having / has
Hao is interested in _____. It would be a win-win situation for both
7. help / helping
the school and Hao.

B Write. Look at the answers. Write the questions.

1. **A** Who _____?

   B Hao has been applying for a job.

2. **A** What _____?

   B He has been looking for a job as a computer technician.

3. **A** Where _____?

   B Hao wants to volunteer at his son's school.

Talk with a partner. Ask and answer the questions.

3 Pronunciation: linking sounds

A Listen to the phrasal verbs. Pay attention to the linking sounds.

CLASS CD2 TK 21

1. clean up
2. think about
3. turn up

4. fill out
5. interested in
6. throw out

7. put on
8. tired of

Listen again and repeat.

B Listen and repeat. Pay attention to the linking sounds in the phrasal verbs.

CLASS CD2 TK 22

1. A What do you need to do?

   B I have to clean up the kitchen.

   A Can I help?

   B Sure. Could you throw out the trash?

   A I'd be happy to.

2. A Don't you think it's cold in here?

   B It's a little cold.

   A Why don't you turn up the heat?

   B That costs too much money. You can put on my jacket.

C Talk with a partner. Practice the conversations. Pay attention to the linking sounds in the phrasal verbs.

1. A Do you need some help?

   B I'm interested in applying for a job here.

   A OK. Just fill out this application, and return it to me.

   B Thanks.

   A Don't forget to put your name on it.

2. A May I help you?

   B I may be interested in buying a big-screen TV.

   A We have some great deals. Let me show you.

   B Thanks, but I'd like to just look around some more.

3. A Do you want to go to a movie tonight?

   B What do you think about just staying home?

   A That's fine. There's a good game on TV.

   B OK. First help me clean up the kitchen. Then we can watch the game.

4. A I want to register for English classes.

   B Fill out this form, please.

   A Can you help me?

   B Sure. I just need to put away these papers.

   A Thank you.

D Write four questions. Use the words in Exercise 3A. Ask your partner. Remember to connect the sounds.

Did you clean up the kitchen last night?

1. _____

2. _____

3. _____

4. _____

LESSON A
Listening

1 Before you listen

A What do you see?

B What is happening?

C What's the story?

1.

2.

Monica

Todd

Unit Goals	**Describe** a crime and suggest solutions
	Write about an emergency
	Interpret a chart about the safest states in the U.S.

2 Listen

STUDENT TK 31
CLASS CD2 TK 23

A **Listen** and answer the questions.

1. Who are the speakers?   2. What are they talking about?

STUDENT TK 31
CLASS CD2 TK 23

B **Listen again.** Take notes. Answer the questions.

1. What happened at Monica and Todd's house?	*someone broke into it*
2. Where were Monica and Todd when the robbery happened?	
3. What did the robber steal?	
4. How has the neighborhood changed?	
5. What does Samantha think they should do?	

3 After you listen

A **Read.** Complete the story.

broke into   come over   crime   got in   mess   robbed   robber   stole

Monica calls Samantha with bad news. While Monica and Todd were out, someone ___broke into___ [1] their home and _____ [2] their TV, DVD player, jewelry, and some cash. Monica is upset because the _____ [3] took her mother's ring. She says the person _____ [4] through a window in the back bedroom.

Samantha is worried. She says they never used to have so much _____ [5] in their neighborhood. She tells Monica that last week someone _____ [6] their neighbor Mr. Purdy, too. Samantha thinks they should start a Neighborhood Watch program. Monica agrees, but first, she needs to clean up the _____ [7] in her house. Samantha offers to _____ [8] and help.

STUDENT TK 32
CLASS CD2 TK 24

Listen and check your answers.

B **Talk** with a partner.

Tell about a crime that happened to you or someone you know.

LESSON B Past continuous

1 Grammar focus: questions and answers

Questions	Answers		
What **was** Beth **doing** yesterday morning?	She **was cleaning** her house.		
What **were** the neighbors **doing** at 10:00?	They **were watching** TV.		
Was Maria **visiting** a neighbor last night?	Yes, she **was**.	No, she **wasn't**.	
Were they **watching** a movie at 8:30?	Yes, they **were**.	No, they **weren't**.	

wasn't = was not
weren't = were not

Turn to page 145 for a complete grammar chart and explanation.

2 Practice

A Write. Complete the sentences. Use the past continuous.

> What were you doing at 8:30 last night?

1. **Roberto and Maya**: We _____*were watching*_____
   (watch)
   a movie at the Rialto Theater.

2. **Mi Young**: I _____ English
   (study)
   at home last night.

3. **Ciro**: I _____ to work.
   (drive)

4. **Magda and Luis**: We _____ dinner at
   (eat)
   Kate's Kitchen Restaurant.

5. **Ilian and Francine**: We _____ a Neighborhood
   (attend)
   Watch meeting.

6. **Susana**: I _____ my grandchildren at my daughter's house.
   (babysit)

7. **Claudia**: I _____ a cake for my daughter's birthday party.
   (bake)

8. **Leila and Mark**: We _____ the kitchen.
   (paint)

 Listen and check your answers.

CLASS CD2 TK 25

112 UNIT 9

B **Talk** with a partner. Look at the picture. Ask and answer questions. Use the past continuous and the verbs in the box.

> **A** What was Bill doing at 7:00 p.m.?
> **B** He was reading.

knit   play a game   read   sew   sleep   talk   watch TV

Write a sentence about each person.

Bill was reading.

3 Communicate

A Work in a small group. Ask and answer questions. Take notes in the chart.

> **A** Sergio, were you at home at 9:00 a.m. yesterday?
> **B** Yes, I was.
> **A** What were you doing?
> **B** I was sleeping.

Name	Time	Action
Sergio	*9:00 a.m.*	*was sleeping*

B **Share** information about your classmates.

LESSON C Past continuous and simple past

1 Grammar focus: adverb clauses with *when* and *while*

> **When** the fire **started**, Maxine and Joel **were sleeping**.
>
> **While** Maxine and Joel **were sleeping**, a fire **started** in the kitchen.

> Maxine and Joel **were sleeping** **when** the fire **started**.
>
> A fire **started** in the kitchen **while** Maxine and Joel **were sleeping**.

Turn to page 148 for a complete grammar chart and explanation.

2 Practice

A **Write.** Complete the sentences. Use the past continuous or simple past.

1. While Dad ___*was working*___ in the
   (work)
   garden, a thief ___*stole*___ his car.
   (steal)

2. I _____ lunch when the fire
   (eat)
   alarm suddenly _____ .
   (go off)

3. Ali _____ off a ladder while
   (fall)
   he _____ the ceiling.
   (paint)

4. When the earthquake _____ , the students _____ a
   (start)   (take)
   test.

5. I _____ a right turn when another car _____ the
   (make)   (hit)
   back of my car.

6. While we _____ , it suddenly _____ to rain.
   (camp)   (begin)

7. Mr. and Mrs. Gomez _____ in the park when a dog
   (jog)
   _____ to chase them.
   (begin)

8. While Diana _____ outside, a stranger _____ up to
   (work)   (drive)
   her house.

Listen and check your answers.

CLASS CD2 TK 26

114 UNIT 9

B **Talk** with a partner. Look at the pictures. Ask and answer questions. Use *when* or *while*.

> **A** What happened?
> **B** While the woman was working, a tree fell on her house.

work	fall	drive	run out of gas
eat	get a parking ticket	cook dinner	the lights go out

Write sentences about what happened.

The woman was working when a tree fell on her house.

3 Communicate

A **Work** with a partner. Describe a situation that happened to you. Answer the questions.

1. What happened?
2. When and where did it happen?
3. What were you doing when it happened?

B **Share** information about your partner.

LESSON D Reading

1 Before you read

Look at the picture. Answer the questions.

1. Who are the people in the picture?
2. What do you think is happening?
3. How do they probably feel?

2 Read

Read the newspaper article. Listen and read again.

STUDENT TK 33
CLASS CD2 TK 27

Home Is More Than a Building
Claypool, AZ

A few months ago, Pedro Ramirez, 45, lost his job in a grocery store. To pay the bills, he got a part-time job at night. Several days later, Pedro's wife, Luisa, gave him a big surprise. She was pregnant with their sixth child. Pedro was happy but worried. "How am I going to support another child without a full-time job?" he wondered.

That evening, Pedro and Luisa got some more news. A fire was coming near their home. By the next morning, the fire was very close. The police ordered every family in the neighborhood to evacuate. The Ramirez family moved quickly. While Pedro was gathering their legal documents, Luisa grabbed the family photographs, and the children put their pets – a cat and a bird – in the family's van. Then, the family drove to the home of Luisa's sister, one hour away.

About 24 hours later, Pedro and Luisa got very bad news. The fire destroyed their home. They lost almost everything. With no home, only part-time work, and a baby coming, Pedro was even more worried about the future.

For the next three months, the Ramirez family stayed with Luisa's sister while workers were rebuilding their home. Many generous people helped them during that difficult time. Friends took them shopping for clothes. Strangers left gifts at their door. A group of children collected $500 to buy bicycles for the Ramirez children.

Because of all the help from friends and neighbors, the Ramirez family was able to rebuild their lives. Two months after the fire, Luisa mailed out holiday cards with this message: "Home is more than a building. Home is wherever there is love."

In a story, time phrases show changes in time.
A few months ago, . . .
Several days later, . . .
That evening, . . .

3 After you read

A **Check** your understanding. Scan the reading. Look for the time phrases. Write numbers to show the order of events.

  _1_ Pedro lost his job.

  _____ Luisa mailed out holiday cards.

  _____ The fire destroyed Pedro and Luisa's home.

  _____ Pedro and Luisa heard about a fire near their home.

  _____ The police ordered people in the neighborhood to evacuate.

  _____ Luisa told Pedro she was pregnant.

  _____ The Ramirez family stayed with Luisa's sister for three months.

B **Build** your vocabulary.

Find the words in the story and underline them. Circle the definitions that best match the reading.

1. support
   a. pay for necessary things
   b. find
   c. say that you agree with someone

2. evacuate
   a. clean
   b. go inside a house
   c. leave a dangerous place

3. gathering
   a. separating
   b. a group of things
   c. collecting

4. grabbed
   a. took quickly
   b. held someone with force
   c. stole

5. destroyed
   a. broke completely
   b. killed
   c. hurt

6. generous
   a. critical
   b. giving
   c. sad

7. strangers
   a. family
   b. friends
   c. people you don't know

8. message
   a. medical treatment
   b. communication
   c. a person who brings things

C **Talk** with a partner. Ask and answer the questions.

1. Tell your partner about an emergency situation that happened to you or your family. What happened?

2. Has someone been generous to you or your family? How?

3. How do you feel about accepting help from strangers?

LESSON E Writing

1 Before you write

A **Talk** with a partner. Think about an emergency. Answer the questions.

1. **Who** did it happen to?
2. **What** happened?
3. **When** did it happen?
4. **Where** did it happen?
5. **Why** or **how** did it happen?

B **Read** the story.

Fire in Our Backyard

One evening last summer, my husband and I were preparing dinner together. My husband was cooking outside, and I was setting the table inside. Suddenly, my husband ran into the kitchen and shouted, "There's a fire in the backyard!" I ran outside and saw fire in the bushes next to our fence. I was really scared because my 70-year-old parents live next door. Luckily, my husband acted quickly. He called the fire department and then started putting water on the fire. The firefighters arrived quickly, and they easily put out the fire. They said a coal from the barbecue started it.

My parents were very surprised when they saw the firefighters. They were watching the news in the living room, and they never knew there was a problem. My father said, "Let's go back and watch the news. Maybe we're on TV!"

Work with a partner. Answer the questions.

1. Who is the story about?
2. When did it happen?
3. Where did it happen?
4. What were the people doing when the story started?
5. What was the emergency?
6. Why was the writer scared?
7. How did the story end?

C **Write** a plan for a story about an emergency that happened to you or someone you know. Answer the questions.

1. Who is the story about?	
2. Where did it happen?	
3. When did it happen?	
4. What were the people doing when the story started?	
5. What was the emergency?	
6. How did the story end?	

2 Write

Write a story about an emergency that happened to you or someone you know. Give the story a title and write a concluding sentence. Use the information from Exercises 1B and 1C to help you.

When you tell a story, answer the questions *Who*, *What*, *When*, *Where*, *Why*, and *How*.

3 After you write

A **Check** your writing.

	Yes	No
1. I gave my story a title.	☐	☐
2. My story answers the questions *Who*, *What*, *When*, *Where*, *Why*, and *How*.	☐	☐
3. I wrote a concluding sentence.	☐	☐

B **Share** your writing with a partner.

1. Take turns. Read your story to a partner.
2. Comment on your partner's story. Ask your partner a question about the story. Tell your partner one thing you learned.

☑ Write a story about an emergency that answers the questions *Who*, *What*, *When*, *Where*, *Why*, and *How*.

LESSON F Another view

1 Life-skills reading

Safest States in the United States			
2007		**2010**	
1	North Dakota	1	New Hampshire
2	Vermont	2	Vermont
3	Maine	3	North Dakota
4	New Hampshire	4	Maine
5	Wyoming	5	Idaho
18	New Jersey	15	New York
20	New York	19	New Jersey
30	Illinois	30	Ohio
39	Texas	36	California
42	California	42	Arizona
43	Florida	43	Maryland

Source: Crime State Rankings 2007 and 2010

A Read the questions. Look at the chart. Fill in the answer.

1. Which state had the same rank in 2007 and 2010?
   - Ⓐ Florida
   - Ⓑ Vermont
   - Ⓒ California
   - Ⓓ New York

2. Which state became less safe in 2010?
   - Ⓐ New York
   - Ⓑ California
   - Ⓒ North Dakota
   - Ⓓ New Hampshire

3. Which state became safer in 2010?
   - Ⓐ Maine
   - Ⓑ Vermont
   - Ⓒ New Jersey
   - Ⓓ New Hampshire

4. Which state had a different rank in 2007 and 2010?
   - Ⓐ North Dakota
   - Ⓑ New Jersey
   - Ⓒ both *a* and *b*
   - Ⓓ neither *a* nor *b*

B Talk with your classmates. Ask and answer the questions.

1. Do you feel safe where you live? Why?
2. Where do you think is the safest place to live?
3. Where do you think is the most dangerous place to live?

2 **Grammar connections:** three uses of the present continuous

Events happening now	Farah **is wearing** new jeans right now.
Ongoing events	I**'m studying** in the library this week.
Events in the near future	Hiro **isn't working** next Saturday.

A **Work** in a small group. Complete the chart.

> **A** What are you doing tonight, Farah?
> **B** I'm studying English.

	Name: _____	Name: _____	Name: _____
1. What are you doing tonight?			
2. What are you looking at right now?			
3. What are you watching on TV this week?			
4. What are you doing next Saturday?			
5. What are you thinking about right now?			
6. What classes are you taking this term?			

B **Work** with a partner. Look at the questions in Exercise 2A. Answer the questions.

1. Which questions are about events happening now? _____
2. Which questions are about ongoing events? _____
3. Which questions are about events in the near future? _____

3 **Wrap up**

Complete the **Self-assessment** on page 140.

☑ Interpret a chart about the safest states in the U.S.;
use the present continuous for three different purposes   **UNIT 9** **121**

LESSON A
Listening

1 **Before you listen**

Talk about the pictures.

A What do you see?

B What is happening?

C What's the story?

Unit Goals

Discuss vacation plans

Read about a tourist attraction

Get information from a hotel advertisement

2 Listen

STUDENT TK 34
CLASS CD2 TK 28

A **Listen** and answer the questions.

1. Who are the speakers?　　　　　2. What are they talking about?

STUDENT TK 34
CLASS CD2 TK 28

B **Listen again.** Complete the chart.

	San Francisco	**Camping**
Transportation	Round-trip airfare per person: $ _____	Gas for the car: $ _____
Lodging	Hotel per night: $ _____　　Tax: _____%	Campsite per night: $ _____

3 After you listen

A **Read.** Complete the story.

book a flight　　days off　　reserve　　tax

camping　　discounts　　round-trip　　tourist

> **CULTURE NOTE**
>
> Advertisements for hotels do not include the room tax. The tax adds 7% to 16% per night to the cost of the room.

Felicia is exhausted. She needs a vacation. Her husband, Ricardo, says he can ask his boss for a few _____days off_____. Felicia would like to go to San Francisco.
                                   1
They look for special travel _____ on the Internet. If they _____ at
                              2   3
least seven days ahead, they can get a _____ ticket for less than $200. On
                                        4
the other hand, hotel room rates will be high because summer is the most popular

_____ season. Also, there is a room _____ on hotel rooms in San
     5   6
Francisco. They figure out that a three-day trip to San Francisco will cost

almost $1,200.

Felicia and her husband decide to change their plans. If they go _____,
                                                                     7
they will save a lot of money and their daughter will have more fun. Felicia's

husband will _____ the campsite after he talks to his boss.
              8

STUDENT TK 35
CLASS CD2 TK 29

Listen and check your answers.

B **Talk** with a partner. Answer the question.

Which would you prefer: a trip to San Francisco or camping in the mountains?

LESSON B Conditionals

1 Grammar focus: future real

> **If** the fare **is** cheap enough, we **will fly**.
>
> **If** the weather **is** bad, she **won't go swimming**.

> We **will fly if** the fare **is** cheap enough.
>
> She **won't go swimming if** the weather **is** bad.

Turn to page 148 for a grammar explanation.

> **USEFUL** LANGUAGE
>
> *won't = will not*

2 Practice

A Write. Complete the sentences. Use the simple present or future form of the verbs. Circle the future conditional clause.

1. Annette and William _____will take_____ their children to Sea Adventure next month
(take)
(if William _____gets_____ a few days off.)
(get)

2. If they _____ a discount, they _____ a room at a hotel.
(get)   (reserve)

3. If prices _____ too high, they _____ an expensive vacation.
(be)   (not / take)

4. We _____ a picnic on Saturday if it _____.
(have)   (not / rain)

5. If you _____ me the money, I _____ the concert tickets.
(give)   (buy)

6. If you _____ to Chicago, we _____ you at the airport.
(come)   (meet)

7. They _____ to Miami next month if they _____ a cheap flight.
(fly)   (find)

8. We _____ camping if the weather _____ too hot.
(not / go)   (be)

Listen and check your answers.

CLASS CD2 TK 30

124 UNIT 10

B **Talk** with a partner. Ask and answer questions about the pictures.

> **A** What will John do if the weather is good?
> **B** He'll play soccer.

> **A** What will he do if the weather isn't good?
> **B** He'll watch a movie.

> **USEFUL** LANGUAGE
> *He'll = He will*

1. John

play soccer   watch a movie

2. Melinda and Pedro

go hiking   go shopping

3. Ken

go swimming   clean the house

4. Andrea

work in the garden   read a book

Write a sentence about each picture.

If the weather is good, John will play soccer.
He'll watch a movie if the weather isn't good.

3 Communicate

A **Work** with a partner. Ask and answer questions. Take notes in the chart.

> **A** What will you do if you have time off in the summer?
> **B** I'll visit my family in Mexico.

1. have time off in the summer	*visit family in Mexico*
2. have a three-day weekend	
3. get some extra money	
4. the weather is beautiful next weekend	

B **Share** information about your partner.

LESSON C Future time clauses

1 Grammar focus: clauses with *before* and *after*

> **Before** Kim **takes** a vacation, he **will finish** school.
>
> **After** Kim **finishes** school, he **will take** a vacation.
>
> Kim **will finish** school **before** he **takes** a vacation.
>
> Kim **will take** a vacation **after** he **finishes** school.
>
> Turn to page 148 for a grammar explanation.

2 Practice

A Write. Complete the sentences. Use the correct form of the verb.

1. Kara _____*will talk*_____ to a travel agent before she _____*books*_____ a flight.
   (talk)   (book)

2. Before Cynthia _____ for Puerto Rico, she _____ some
   (leave)   (buy)

   new clothes.

3. Donald _____ a taxi to the hotel after he _____ his baggage.
   (take)   (pick up)

4. The campers _____ a fire before they _____ their dinner.
   (make)   (cook)

5. After they _____ eating, they _____ the campsite.
   (finish)   (clean up)

6. I _____ you after I _____ from my trip.
   (call)   (return)

7. After I _____ my passport, I _____ the reservations.
   (get)   (make)

8. Before we _____ to Mexico, we _____ some words in Spanish.
   (go)   (learn)

9. Jack _____ the doors before he _____ for the airport.
   (lock)   (leave)

Listen and check your answers.

B **Talk** with a partner. Anita is going to the airport. Talk about her plans. Use *before* or *after*.

> **A** After Anita checks in, she'll go through security.
> **B** Before Anita goes through security, she'll check in.

1. check in

2. go through security

3. buy a cup of coffee

4. read a newspaper

5. get on the plane

6. turn off her cell phone

Write sentences about Anita. Use *before* and *after*.

Anita will go through security after she checks in.

3 Communicate

A **Imagine** you are going to take a weekend trip. Choose the location. Write three things you need to do before the trip.

B **Interview** a partner. Take notes in the chart.

> **A** Where will you go on your trip?
> **B** To the mountains.
> **A** What will you do first?
> **B** I'll reserve a campsite.
> **A** What will you do after you reserve a campsite?
> **B** I'll pack warm clothes.
> **A** What will you do after that?
> **B** I'll pack my camping supplies.

C **Share** information about your partner.

You
Location:
1. _____
2. _____
3. _____
Your partner
Location:
1. _____
2. _____
3. _____

LESSON **D** Reading

1 Before you read

Look at the picture. Answer the questions.

1. What do you see on the postcard?
2. Would you like to visit this place? Why or why not?

2 Read

STUDENT TK 36
CLASS CD2 TK 32

Read the article from a tourist guidebook. Listen and read again.

The ROCK SAN FRANCISCO'S BIGGEST TOURIST ATTRACTION

Alcatraz, a small, rocky island in the middle of San Francisco Bay, was once the most famous prison in the United States. For a period of 29 years, from 1934 to 1963, over 1,500 dangerous criminals lived in the prison's 378 cells. People believed that it was impossible to escape from Alcatraz Island. However, in 1962, two brothers, John and Clarence Anglin, and another man named Frank Morris, escaped on a raft made of raincoats. A famous movie, *Escape from Alcatraz*, tells this amazing story. Other famous prisoners who lived on the island included Al Capone, the gangster, and Robert Stroud, the "Birdman of Alcatraz."

Alcatraz prison closed in 1963. The island became a national park, and since then it has been a major attraction for tourists from all over the world. These days, many people call Alcatraz by its popular name, "The Rock."

In the summer, it is wise to buy tickets to the island in advance because the ferries sell out. Evening tours are less crowded. The admission prices listed include the ferry, tickets, and an audio tour.

General admission	
Adult (18–61)	$36.00
Junior (12–17)	$34.50
Child (5–11)	$26.00
Senior (62+)	$34.50

> Words between commas sometimes explain the words before them.
>
> *For a period of 29 years, from 1934 to 1963, . . .*

3 After you read

A **Check** your understanding.

1. What is Alcatraz?
2. Why did dangerous criminals go to Alcatraz?
3. What happened in 1962?
4. How long has Alcatraz been a tourist attraction?
5. How much is admission for a ten-year-old child?
6. How much is admission for a three-year-old child?

B **Build** your vocabulary.

1. Find the following words in the reading. Underline them.

admission	cells	ferries	prison
attraction	escape	in advance	sell out

2. Work with a partner. Guess the meaning of the words. Note the clues that helped you. Then use a dictionary to check your guesses.

> I guess that *attraction* means a place tourists want to visit. My clue was the phrase "biggest tourist attraction" in the title. The dictionary definition of *attraction [noun]* is "a thing or place that tourists like to see or visit."

3. Complete the sentences. Use the words from Exercise B1.

   a. The Empire State Building in New York is a famous tourist _____.

   b. General _____ to the museum is $36.00 for adults.

   c. Tickets to popular music concerts often _____ very quickly.

   d. We bought our tickets six months _____.

   e. To get to the Ellis Island Immigration Museum in New York, you have to take one of the _____ from Manhattan.

   f. Alcatraz used to be a _____. Then it became a national park.

   g. Each prisoner in Alcatraz lived in one of the 378 _____.

   h. Thirty-six men tried to _____ from Alcatraz.

C **Talk** with a partner. Ask and answer the questions.

1. Tell about a popular tourist attraction in a city you have visited. What was the cost of admission?
2. What kinds of tickets do you usually buy in advance?
3. Have you ever taken a ferry ride? Where did you go?

☑ Read an article about a tourist attraction; guess the meaning of words from context clues **UNIT 10** **129**

LESSON E Writing

1 Before you write

A **Work** with a partner. Write the name of a tourist attraction in your community. Make a list of things to do or see there.

Attraction: _____

1. _____
2. _____
3. _____

B **Read** the paragraph.

COUNTY FAIRS

One of the biggest tourist attractions in many cities in the United States is the county fair. A fair has something for everyone. It has a beautiful flower show and a photography exhibit. If you have children, they will love the Ferris wheel and the fast rides. If you like animals, you can watch many different animal competitions. The winner in each competition gets a blue ribbon. A fair also has displays of new products, such as cleaning products and cooking tools. When you get hungry, you can buy food from one of the many booths. After you have eaten dinner, you can listen to a concert of live music until late in the evening. Many fairs end with spectacular fireworks. There really is something for everyone at a fair.

C **Complete** the outline. Write five examples of things to do at the county fair.

Topic sentence: *A fair has something for everyone.*

Examples:

1. _____

   _____

2. _____

   _____

3. _____

   _____

4. _____

   _____

5. _____

   _____

> Use complex sentences to make your writing more interesting. Complex sentences are sentences with a dependent clause.
>
> *If you have children, they will love the Ferris wheel and the fast rides.*
>
> *When you get hungry, you can buy food from at least 25 different booths.*

Conclusion: *There really is something for everyone at a fair.*

D **Work** with a partner. Look at the paragraph in Exercise 1B. Find four complex sentences. Underline them.

2 Write

Write a paragraph about a tourist attraction in your city. Include the topic sentence, at least three examples, and a conclusion. Use at least two complex sentences in your paragraph. Before you write, make an outline. Use Exercises 1B and 1C to help you.

3 After you write

A **Check** your writing.

	Yes	No
1. My paragraph has a topic sentence and a conclusion.	☐	☐
2. My paragraph has at least three examples.	☐	☐
3. My paragraph has complex sentences with *before*, *after*, *when*, or *if*.	☐	☐

B **Share** your writing with a partner.

1. Take turns. Read your paragraph to a partner.
2. Comment on your partner's paragraph. Ask your partner a question about the paragraph. Tell your partner one thing you learned.

LESSON **F** Another view

Gateway Inn

524 Memorial Highway
Orlando, Florida
407-555-7000

Amenities	Restaurant in lobby (kids eat free), outdoor pool, fitness center, golf nearby, free transportation to local theme parks
Distance from destinations	Theme parks (3.5 miles)
Room rates	Budget: $89–$100 Standard: $130–$160 Deluxe: $200–$250
Room tax	12%

Western Universal Inn

4617 Southland Rd.
Orlando, Florida
407-555-9100

Amenities	Breakfast buffet, outdoor pool, self-parking (free), in-room safe, iron, hair dryer, Internet access
Distance from destinations	Daytona Beach (47 miles), International Drive (1 mile), Winter Park (8 miles), Theme parks (12 miles)
Room rates	Budget: $130–$165 Standard: $160–$175 Deluxe: $250–$300
Room tax	12%

A **Read** the questions. Look at the hotel information. Fill in the answer.

1. What is the rate for a standard room at the Gateway Inn?

   Ⓐ $89–$100

   Ⓑ $130–$160

   Ⓒ $160–$175

   Ⓓ $200–$250

2. Where can children eat for free?

   Ⓐ Daytona Beach

   Ⓑ Gateway Inn

   Ⓒ Western Universal Inn

   Ⓓ none of the above

3. How far is the Western Universal Inn from the theme parks?

   Ⓐ 3.5 miles

   Ⓑ 8 miles

   Ⓒ 10 miles

   Ⓓ 12 miles

4. Where is self-parking free?

   Ⓐ Gateway Inn

   Ⓑ Western Universal Inn

   Ⓒ neither *a* nor *b*

   Ⓓ both *a* and *b*

B **Talk** with a partner. Ask and answer the questions.

Which hotel do you prefer? Why?

2 Grammar connections: three uses of the present perfect

Events that began in the past and continue to now	Keiko **has taken** English classes for six years.
Events that have happened before now (time unclear)	Jason **has been** to Canada.
Events that were repeated before now	I **have flown** on a plane six times.

A Talk with your classmates. Complete the chart.

> **A** Have you been to another country on vacation, Elena?
> **B** No, I haven't.
> **A** Have you been to another country on vacation, Jason?
> **C** Yes, I have. I've been to Canada.

Find someone who . . .	Name
has been to another country on vacation.	
has taken English classes for more than five years.	
hasn't missed a class since the beginning of the term.	
hasn't changed his/her hairstyle in the last five years.	
has flown on a plane more than once.	
has seen snow.	
has shopped online a lot recently.	
hasn't sent a text message in the last 24 hours.	
has lived in the same place for more than ten years.	
has lived in this country for less than a year.	
hasn't traveled by bus before.	

B Share information about your classmates.

> Jason has been to Canada on vacation.

> Keiko has taken English classes for six years.

3 Wrap up

Complete the **Self-assessment** on page 140.

☑ Interpret hotel information in an ad; use the present perfect for three different purposes **UNIT 10**

Review

1 Listening

CLASS CD2 TK 33

Listen. Put a check (✓) under *Yes* or *No*.

	Yes	No
1. Brad Spencer was missing for two nights.		✓
2. He disappeared Sunday.		
3. He was camping with his friends.		
4. He was wearing only a T-shirt and shorts.		
5. When the park police found him, he was playing his guitar.		
6. If Brad returns to the park, he's going to stay on the trails.		

Talk with a partner. Check your answers.

2 Grammar

A Write. Complete the story. Use the correct words.

A Problem in Chicago

Tina Foster is visiting Chicago for the first time. While she _____*was taking*_____

1. took / was taking

a walk in Lincoln Park early this morning, she _____ her wallet

2. lost / was losing

with all her cash, identification, and credit cards. When she got back to her hotel, she

realized that her wallet _____. She is going to _____

3. missed / was missing   4. search / searching

the park. If she _____ her wallet, she _____

5. doesn't find / didn't find   6. calls / will call

the credit card companies. After she _____ her credit cards, she

7. cancels / canceled

_____ to the nearest police station and file a police report.

8. will go / goes

B Write. Look at the answers. Write the questions.

1. **A** Who _____?

   B Tina Foster is visiting Chicago for the first time.

2. **A** What _____?

   B Tina was taking a walk when she lost her wallet.

3. **A** Where _____?

   B She will file a police report at the nearest police station.

Talk with a partner. Ask and answer the questions.

134   REVIEW: UNITS 9 & 10

3 Pronunciation: unstressed vowel

A **Listen** to the unstressed vowel sounds in these words. Unstressed vowels sound like "uh."

CLASS CD2 TK 34

1. up-sét
2. a-bóut
3. fá-mi-ly
4. éx-tra
5. trá-vel

6. po-líce
7. va-cá-tion
8. dán-ge-rous
9. Sa-mán-tha
10. phó-to-graphs

The unstressed vowels are in **green**.

Listen again and repeat.

B **Listen and repeat.** Then underline the unstressed vowels in these words.

CLASS CD2 TK 35

1. Samantha is upset.
2. Where's the travel agent?
3. The prison is dangerous.
4. It's about seven o'clock.

5. Did you take photographs?
6. Call the police!
7. She'll think about visiting her family.
8. I need a vacation.

Talk with a partner. Compare your answers.

C **Talk** with a partner. Practice the conversations. Pay attention to the unstressed vowel sounds in **green**.

1. **A** There was a lot of excitement at the Community Adult School yesterday!

   B What are you talking about?

   A There was a fire in the kitchen!

   B Did the fire department come?

   A Yes. A student heard the smoke alarm and called 911 right away.

2. **A** Betty is going to Washington next week!

   B Are you serious? Won't that cost a lot?

   A Well, she probably got a cheap ticket.

   B Is she traveling with her family?

   A No. Her husband's going to take care of the children.

D **Write** five questions. Use the words in Exercise 3A. Ask a partner your questions. Remember to pay attention to the unstressed vowel sound.

What makes you get upset?

1. _____
2. _____
3. _____
4. _____
5. _____

Self-assessments

UNIT 1 Personal information

A   **Vocabulary** Write eight new words you have learned.

_____   _____   _____   _____

_____   _____   _____   _____

B   **Skills and functions** Read the sentences. Rate yourself. Circle 3 (*I agree.*) OR 2 (*I'm not sure.*) OR 1 (*I can't do this.*).

I can ask and answer questions using verbs + gerunds: ***Do*** you **enjoy dancing**? *I* **love dancing**.	3 2 1
I can use **more than**, **less than**, and **as much as** to compare likes and interests: *I like reading* **more than** *watching TV.*	3 2 1
I can use **must** for logical conclusions: *Ella isn't answering her phone. She* **must be** *busy.*	3 2 1
I can predict what I am going to read by looking at the title and pictures.	3 2 1
I can write a paragraph with a topic sentence and supporting details.	3 2 1

C   **What's next?** Choose one.

☐ I am ready for the unit test.   ☐ I need more practice with _____.

UNIT 2 At school

A   **Vocabulary** Write eight new words you have learned.

_____   _____   _____   _____

_____   _____   _____   _____

B   **Skills and functions** Read the sentences. Rate yourself. Circle 3 (*I agree.*) OR 2 (*I'm not sure.*) OR 1 (*I can't do this.*).

I can ask and answer present perfect questions with **How long**, **for**, and **since**: **How long has** *he* **been** *here? He* **has been** *here* **for two years** / **since January**.	3 2 1
I can ask and answer present perfect *Yes / No* questions with **ever**: **Have** *you* **ever studied** *French? No, I* **haven't**.	3 2 1
I can distinguish between simple past and present perfect: *She* **moved** *to Chicago in 2008. She* **has lived** *in Chicago for six years.*	3 2 1
I can find examples in a reading.	3 2 1
I can write a paragraph that uses examples to support my ideas.	3 2 1

C   **What's next?** Choose one.

☐ I am ready for the unit test.   ☐ I need more practice with _____.

UNIT 3 Friends and family

A **Vocabulary** Write eight new words you have learned.

_____ _____ _____ _____

_____ _____ _____ _____

B **Skills and functions** Read the sentences. Rate yourself. Circle 3 (*I agree.*) OR 2 (*I'm not sure.*) OR 1 (*I can't do this.*).

I can give reasons using **because of** and **because**: *I can't reach the smoke alarm **because of** the high ceiling.* **Because** *the ceiling is high, I can't reach the smoke alarm.*	3 2 1
I can use **too** and **enough**: *The ceiling is **too high**. He **isn't tall enough** to reach the ceiling.*	3 2 1
I can use **be able to** to talk about ability: *Jose **is able to play** the guitar.*	3 2 1
I can identify the main idea, facts, and examples in a reading.	3 2 1
I can write a letter of complaint.	3 2 1

C **What's next?** Choose one.

☐ I am ready for the unit test.   ☐ I need more practice with _____.

UNIT 4 Health

A **Vocabulary** Write eight new words you have learned.

_____ _____ _____ _____

_____ _____ _____ _____

B **Skills and functions** Read the sentences. Rate yourself. Circle 3 (*I agree.*) OR 2 (*I'm not sure.*) OR 1 (*I can't do this.*).

I can ask and answer questions using the present perfect with **lately** and **recently**: **Have** *you **gained** weight **recently**? No, I **have lost** weight **lately**.*	3 2 1
I can ask and answer questions with **used to**: **Did** *you **use to** exercise? I **used to** exercise a lot, but now I don't.*	3 2 1
I can report commands using **tell**: *She **told us to walk** quickly.*	3 2 1
I can identify the topic of a text by reading the introduction and conclusion.	3 2 1
I can write a paragraph with a topic sentence.	3 2 1

C **What's next?** Choose one.

☐ I am ready for the unit test.   ☐ I need more practice with _____.

UNIT 5 Around town

A **Vocabulary** Write eight new words you have learned.

_____   _____   _____   _____

_____   _____   _____   _____

B **Skills and functions** Read the sentences. Rate yourself. Circle 3 (*I agree.*) OR
2 (*I'm not sure.*) OR 1 (*I can't do this.*).

I can use verbs + infinitives in questions and answers: *Where do you **plan to go**? I **plan to go** to the park.*	3 2 1
I can ask and answer questions using the present perfect with **already** and **yet**: **Have** you **already bought** the tickets? No, I **haven't bought** them **yet**.	3 2 1
I can use verbs + infinitives and verbs + gerunds: *I **want to go** to the mall. I **enjoy going** to the mall.*	3 2 1
I can guess if a word has a positive or negative meaning.	3 2 1
I can use an informal writing style in an e-mail.	3 2 1

C **What's next?** Choose one.

☐ I am ready for the unit test.   ☐ I need more practice with _____.

UNIT 6 Time

A **Vocabulary** Write eight new words you have learned.

_____   _____   _____   _____

_____   _____   _____   _____

B **Skills and functions** Read the sentences. Rate yourself. Circle 3 (*I agree.*) OR
2 (*I'm not sure.*) OR 1 (*I can't do this.*).

I can use adverb clauses with **when**: **When** she **feels** tired, she **takes** a break.	3 2 1
I can use adverb clauses with **before** and **after**: **Before** she **eats**, she **reads**. She **eats after** she **reads**.	3 2 1
I can use **one**, **some**, **any**, **it**, and **them** to refer to nouns: *Do you have <u>a pencil</u>? Sure. Here's **one**.* *Did you read <u>the e-mails</u>? Yes, I read **them**.*	3 2 1
I can identify a definition, an explanation, or an example in a reading.	3 2 1
I can use words and phrases to signal the conclusion of my paragraph.	3 2 1

C **What's next?** Choose one.

☐ I am ready for the unit test.   ☐ I need more practice with _____.

UNIT 7 Shopping

A **Vocabulary** Write eight new words you have learned.

_____   _____   _____   _____

_____   _____   _____   _____

B **Skills and functions** Read the sentences. Rate yourself. Circle 3 (*I agree.*) OR
2 (*I'm not sure.*) OR 1 (*I can't do this.*).

I can make suggestions using **could** and give advice using **should**: You **could get** a smaller car. You **should open** a savings account.	3 2 1
I can use gerunds after prepositions in questions and statements: What are you interested **in doing**? I'm interested **in cooking**.	3 2 1
I can use collocations with **get** and **take**: Janet **got laid off**. Then she **took a vacation**.	3 2 1
I can identify problems and solutions in a reading.	3 2 1
I can use words like **first**, **second**, and **finally** to list my ideas.	3 2 1

C **What's next?** Choose one.

☐ I am ready for the unit test.   ☐ I need more practice with _____.

UNIT 8 Work

A **Vocabulary** Write eight new words you have learned.

_____   _____   _____

_____   _____   _____

B **Skills and functions** Read the sentences. Rate yourself. Circle 3 (*I agree.*) OR
2 (*I'm not sure.*) OR 1 (*I can't do this.*).

I can ask and answer questions using the present perfect continuous: How long **have** you **been living** here? I **have been living** here for a long time.	3 2 1
I can use separable phrasal verbs: He **handed out** the papers. He **handed** them **out**.	3 2 1
I can distinguish between the present continuous and the present perfect continuous: Mark **is reading** a book right now. I**'ve been reading** this magazine for an hour.	3 2 1
I can scan a reading for specific information.	3 2 1
I can write a thank-you letter.	3 2 1

C **What's next?** Choose one.

☐ I am ready for the unit test.   ☐ I need more practice with _____.

UNIT 9 Daily living

A **Vocabulary** Write eight new words you have learned.

_____   _____   _____   _____

_____   _____   _____   _____

B **Skills and functions** Read the sentences. Rate yourself. Circle 3 (*I agree.*) OR 2 (*I'm not sure.*) OR 1 (*I can't do this.*).

I can use the past continuous in questions and answers: *What **were** you **doing** yesterday morning? I **was watching** TV.*	3 2 1
I can use **while** with the past continuous and **when** with the simple past: ***While** I **was sleeping**, the fire **started**. **When** the fire **started**, I **was sleeping**.*	3 2 1
I can use the present continuous in three ways: *Tom **is sleeping** right now. Chu **is living** with his parents. Omar **isn't coming** to the party tomorrow.*	3 2 1
I can use time phrases in a reading to sequence events.	3 2 1
I can write a paragraph with details answering *Wh-* questions.	3 2 1

C **What's next?** Choose one.

☐ I am ready for the unit test.   ☐ I need more practice with _____ .

UNIT 10 Free time

A **Vocabulary** Write eight new words you have learned.

_____   _____   _____   _____

_____   _____   _____   _____

B **Skills and functions** Read the sentences. Rate yourself. Circle 3 (*I agree.*) OR 2 (*I'm not sure.*) OR 1 (*I can't do this.*).

I can use future real conditionals with **if**: *I **will fly if** the fare **is** cheap.*	3 2 1
I can use future time clauses with **before** and **after**: *He'll **finish** school **before** he **finds** a job. **After** he **finishes** school, he'll **find** a job.*	3 2 1
I can use present perfect in three ways: *Mohamed **has lived** in Miami for a year. Luz **has been** to Miami. I **have visited** Miami three times.*	3 2 1
I can find the explanation of words in a reading.	3 2 1
I can use complex sentences in writing.	3 2 1

C **What's next?** Choose one.

☐ I am ready for the unit test.   ☐ I need more practice with _____ .

Reference

Verbs + gerunds

A gerund is the base form of a verb + -*ing*. Gerunds often follow verbs that talk about preferences. Use a gerund like a noun: *I love* _dancing_.

Spelling rules for gerunds

- For verbs ending in a vowel-consonant pair, repeat the consonant before adding -*ing*:
  stop → *stopping*   *get* → *getting*
- For verbs ending in silent -*e*, drop the *e* before -*ing*:
  dance → *dancing*   *exercise* → *exercising*

  but:

  be → *being*   *see* → *seeing*

Questions

Do / Does		
Do	I	
	you	
	we	
	they	enjoy dancing?
Does	he	
	she	
	it	

Affirmative statements

I		
You	enjoy	
We		
They		dancing.
He		
She	enjoys	
It		

Negative statements

I		
You	don't enjoy	
We		
They		dancing.
He		
She	doesn't enjoy	
It		

Verbs gerunds often follow

avoid	feel like	love	quit
can't help	finish	mind	recommend
dislike	hate	miss	regret
enjoy	like	practice	suggest

Gerunds after prepositions

Prepositions are words like *in*, *of*, *about*, and *for*. Prepositions are often used in phrases with adjectives (*excited about*, *interested in*) and verbs (*think about*). Gerunds often follow these phrases.

Wh- questions: *What*

What			
What	am	I	
	are	you	
		we	
		they	tired of doing?
		he	
	is	she	
		it	

Affirmative statements

I	am	
You		
We	are	
They		tired of working.
He		
She	is	
It		

Phrases gerunds often follow

afraid of	famous for	nervous about	thank (someone) for
amazed by	good at	plan on	think about
angry at	happy about	pleased about	tired of
bad at	interested in	sad about	worried about
excited about	look forward to	talk about	

Verbs + infinitives

An infinitive is *to* + the base form of a verb. Infinitives often follow verbs that talk about future ideas. See below for a list of verbs that infinitives often follow.

Wh- questions: *Where*

Where	do	I	want to go?
		you	
		we	
		they	
	does	he	
		she	
		it	

Affirmative statements

I	want to go	to the park.
You		
We		
They		
He	wants to go	
She		
It		

Yes / No questions

Do	I	want to go?
	you	
	we	
	they	
Does	he	
	she	
	it	

Short answers

Yes,	I	do.
	you	
	we	
	they	
	he	does.
	she	
	it	

No,	I	don't.
	you	
	we	
	they	
	he	doesn't.
	she	
	it	

don't   = do not
doesn't = does not

Verbs infinitives often follow

agree	hope	need	promise
can / can't afford	intend	offer	refuse
decide	learn	plan	volunteer
expect	manage	prepare	want
help	mean	pretend	would like

Present perfect

The present perfect is *have* or *has* + past participle. Use the present perfect to talk about actions that started in the past and continue to now. See page 146 for a list of past participles with irregular verbs.

Use *how long* + present perfect to ask about length of time.
Use *for* with a period of time to answer questions with *how long*.
Use *since* with a point in time to answer questions with *how long*.

Wh- questions: *How long*

| How long | have | I / you / we / they | been | here? |
| | has | he / she / it | been | |

Affirmative statements: *for* and *since*

| I / You / We / They | have been | here | for two hours. |
| He / She / It | has been | | since 6:00 p.m. |

Use *ever* with the present perfect to ask *Yes / No* questions about things that happened at any time before now.

| haven't | = | have not |
| hasn't | = | has not |

Yes / No questions: *ever*

| Have | you / we / they | ever | been late? |
| Has | he / she / it | ever | been late? |

Short answers

| Yes, | you / we / they | have. |
| Yes, | he / she / it | has. |

| No, | you / we / they | haven't. |
| No, | he / she / it | hasn't. |

Use *recently* and *lately* with the present perfect to talk about things that happened in the very recent past, not very long ago.

Yes / No questions: *recently* and *lately*

| Have | I / you / we / they | been | early recently? |
| Has | he / she / it | | early lately? |

Use *already* and *yet* with the present perfect to talk about actions based on expectations.

Affirmative statements: *already*

| I / You / We / They | have | already | eaten. |
| He / She / It | has | | |

Negative statements: *yet*

| I / You / We / They | haven't | eaten | yet. |
| He / She / It | hasn't | | |

Present perfect continuous

The present perfect continuous is *have* or *has* + *been* + present participle. Use the present perfect continuous to talk about actions that started in the past, continue to now, and will probably continue in the future.

Yes / No questions

Have	I / you / we / they	been sitting here for a long time?
Has	he / she / it	

Short answers

Yes,	I / you / we / they	have.	
	he / she / it	has.	

No,	I / you / we / they	haven't.	
	he / she / it	hasn't.	

Wh- questions: *How long*

How long	have	I / you / we / they	been sitting here?
	has	he / she / it	

Affirmative statements: *for* and *since*

I / You / We / They	have been sitting here	for an hour. since 10 a.m.
He / She / It	has been sitting here	

used to

Used to talks about things that happened in the past. Use *used to* to talk about a past situation or past habit that is not true now.

Yes / No questions

Did	I / you / we / they / he / she / it	use to arrive late?

Short answers

Yes,	I / you / we / they / he / she / it	did.

No,	I / you / we / they / he / she / it	didn't.

didn't = did not

Affirmative statements

I / You / We / They / He / She / It	used to arrive late.

Past continuous

Use the past continuous to talk about actions that were happening at a specific time in the past. The actions were not completed at that time.

Wh- questions: What

What	was	I	doing last night?
	were	you	
		we	
		they	
	was	he	
		she	
		it	

Affirmative statements

I	was	working.
You	were	
We		
They		
He	was	
She		
It		

Yes / No questions

Was	I	working?
Were	you	
	we	
	they	
Was	he	
	she	
	it	

Short answers

Yes,	I	was.
	you	were.
	we	
	they	
	he	was.
	she	
	it	

No,	I	wasn't.
	you	weren't.
	we	
	they	
	he	wasn't.
	she	
	it	

wasn't = was not
weren't = were not

could and should

Use *could* to give suggestions. Use *should* to give advice. *Should* gives stronger advice than *could*.

Wh- questions: What

What	could should	I	do?
		you	
		we	
		they	
		he	
		she	
		it	

Affirmative statements

I	could should	go home.
You		
We		
They		
He		
She		
It		

Negative statements

I	couldn't shouldn't	go home.
You		
We		
They		
He		
She		
It		

couldn't = could not
shouldn't = should not

Irregular verbs

Base form	Simple past	Past participle	Base form	Simple past	Past participle
be	was / were	been	leave	left	left
become	became	become	lose	lost	lost
begin	began	begun	make	made	made
break	broke	broken	meet	met	met
bring	brought	brought	pay	paid	paid
build	built	built	put	put	put
buy	bought	bought	read	read	read
catch	caught	caught	ride	rode	ridden
choose	chose	chosen	run	ran	run
come	came	come	say	said	said
cost	cost	cost	see	saw	seen
cut	cut	cut	sell	sold	sold
do	did	done	send	sent	sent
drink	drank	drunk	set	set	set
drive	drove	driven	show	showed	shown
eat	ate	eaten	sing	sang	sung
fall	fell	fallen	sit	sat	sat
feel	felt	felt	sleep	slept	slept
fight	fought	fought	speak	spoke	spoken
find	found	found	spend	spent	spent
fly	flew	flown	stand	stood	stood
forget	forgot	forgotten	steal	stole	stolen
get	got	gotten / got	swim	swam	swum
give	gave	given	take	took	taken
go	went	gone	teach	taught	taught
have	had	had	tell	told	told
hear	heard	heard	think	thought	thought
hide	hid	hidden	throw	threw	thrown
hit	hit	hit	understand	understood	understood
hold	held	held	wake	woke	woken
hurt	hurt	hurt	wear	wore	worn
keep	kept	kept	win	won	won
know	knew	known	write	wrote	written

Spelling rules for regular past participles

- To form the past participle of regular verbs, add -ed to the base form:
  listen → listened

- For regular verbs ending in a consonant + -y, change y to i and add -ed:
  study → studied

- For regular verbs ending in a vowel + -y, add -ed:
  play → played

- For regular verbs ending in -e, add -d:
  live → lived

Grammar explanations

Separable phrasal verbs

A phrasal verb is a verb + preposition. The meaning of the phrasal verb is different from the meaning of the verb alone.

He *handed out* the papers to the class. = He *gave* the papers to the class.

A separable phrasal verb can have a noun between the verb and the preposition.

He *handed **the papers** out*.

A separable phrasal verb can have a pronoun between the verb and the preposition.

He *handed **them** out*.

Common separable phrasal verbs

call back	cut off	find out	look up	throw away / out
call up	do over	give back	pick out	turn down
clean up	fill in	hand in	put away / back	turn off
cross out	fill out	hand out	shut off	turn up
cut down	fill up	leave on	tear up	

Comparisons

Use *more than*, *less than*, and *as much as* to compare nouns and gerunds. A gerund is the base form of a verb + *-ing*. It is often used as a noun. You can compare activities by using gerunds and *more than*, *less than*, and *as much as*.

I enjoy *walking more than driving*.

She likes *cooking less than eating*.

They enjoy *singing as much as dancing*.

Giving reasons and explanations with *because of* phrases and *because* clauses

Use a *because of* phrase or a *because* clause to give an explanation. A *because of* phrase is the part of the sentence that begins with *because of* and has a noun phrase. A *because* clause is the part of the sentence that begins with *because* and has a subject and verb. Use a comma (,) when the *because of* phrase or *because* clause begins the sentence.

I came to Ohio *because of my children*.
Because of my children, I came to Ohio.

I came to Ohio *because my children are here*.
Because my children are here, I came to Ohio.

Adjectives with *too* and *enough*

Use *too* + adjective to talk about more than the right amount.

The ladder is *too tall*.

Use adjective + *enough* to talk about the right amount of something.

The ladder is *tall enough* to reach the ceiling.

Use *not* + adjective + *enough* to talk about less than the right amount.

The ladder is *not tall enough*.

Capitalization rules

Capitalize the first, last, and other important words in titles.	**M**y **S**trategies for **L**earning **E**nglish **S**alsa **S**tarz at **C**entury **P**ark **E**scape from **A**lcatraz
Capitalize letters in abbreviations.	**TV** (television) **DVD** (digital video disc or digital versatile disc) **ATM** (automated teller machine or automatic teller machine)
Capitalize titles when they follow a name.	Latisha Holmes, **P**resident, Rolling Hills Neighborhood Watch Janice Hill, **P**ersonnel **M**anager, Smart Shop

Adverb clauses

A clause is a part of a sentence that has a subject and a verb. A dependent clause often begins with time words such as *when*, *before*, and *after*. The dependent clause can come at the beginning or end of a sentence. Use a comma (,) after a dependent clause that comes at the beginning of a sentence. Do not use a comma when a dependent clause comes at the end of a sentence.

when: Use *when* + present time verbs to talk about habits.

> *When I have a lot to do*, I make a to-do list.
> I make a to-do list *when I have a lot to do*.

before: Use *before* to order events in a sentence. *Before* introduces the second event.

Use *before* with the simple present to talk about habits.

> First, she reads the newspaper. Second, she eats breakfast. =
> She reads the newspaper *before she eats breakfast*.
> *Before she eats breakfast*, she reads the newspaper.

Use *before* with the simple present and future to talk about future plans.

> First, he'll finish school. Second, he'll take a vacation. =
> He'll finish school *before he takes a vacation*.
> *Before he takes a vacation*, he'll finish school.

after: Use *after* to order events in a sentence. *After* introduces the first event.

Use *after* with the simple present to talk about habits.

> First, I eat dinner. Second, I watch the news. =
> I watch the news *after I eat dinner*.
> *After I eat dinner*, I watch the news.

Use *after* with the simple present and future to talk about future plans.

> First, he'll finish school. Second, he'll take a vacation. =
> He'll take a vacation *after he finishes school*.
> *After he finishes school*, he'll take a vacation.

when and **while**: Use *when* or *while* with the past continuous and simple past to show that one past action interrupted another past action.

Use *when* with the simple past for the action that interrupted.

> They were sleeping *when the fire started*.
> *When the fire started*, they were sleeping.

Use *while* with the past continuous to show the action that was happening before the interruption.

> The fire started *while they were sleeping*.
> *While they were sleeping*, the fire started.

if: Use *if* clauses to talk about future possibility. Use the simple present in the clause with *if*. Use the future in the other clause to talk about what could happen.

> She won't go *if the weather is bad*.
> *If the weather is bad*, she won't go.

Self-study audio script

Welcome

Page 3, Exercise 2A – Track 2

A Hi, Silvia. What do you want to do in the future?

B I want to open my own beauty salon someday.

A What steps do you need to take?

B First, I need to go to beauty school for two years.

A What's the next step after that?

B Second, I need to take an exam to get my license.

A And after that?

B Third, I need to work in a salon to get experience.

A That sounds great. Do you have any other goals?

B I hope to become a business owner in five years. I don't want to work for anyone else.

Page 4, Exercise 3A – Track 3

1. Javier Molina works at a grocery store.
2. He puts groceries in bags for customers.
3. Javier is working at the store right now.
4. He is helping a woman with her bags of groceries.
5. He is talking to the woman.
6. He works every day from 9 a.m. to 5 p.m.
7. He likes his job, but he wants to do something different in the future.
8. Javier is going to cooking school at night.
9. He wants to be a chef at a restaurant.
10. He is planning to graduate from cooking school in six months.

Page 4, Exercise 3B – Track 4

Oksana Petrova is from Russia. She is living in Philadelphia right now. She works at an elementary school. She has a job as a teacher's assistant. She is working at the school right now. She is helping the students with math at the moment.

Oksana wants to become a teacher in the U.S. She studies English every evening. She plans to take elementary education classes at the community college next year. She is saving her money right now, because college classes are very expensive. She also is looking for another part-time job. She needs to pay her bills every month.

Page 5, Exercises 4A and 4B – Track 5

1. Diego Mata moved to the United States in 2005.
2. He got a job at a gas station.

3. He also took classes in English and auto mechanics.
4. Diego will finish his classes in auto mechanics next month.
5. He will look for a job when he is finished.
6. Diego liked his job at the gas station.
7. He will also like working as a mechanic.
8. He lived in an apartment last year.
9. He will move to a house next year.
10. He will also get married next summer.

Page 5, Exercise 4C – Track 6

1. **A** When did you move to this city?
   B I moved here in 2011.
2. **A** How long will you stay here?
   B Maybe I will stay here for one more year.
3. **A** Where did you live before you moved here?
   B I lived in Taiwan.
4. **A** How long will you study English in the future?
   B I will study English for two more years.

Unit 1: Personal information

Page 7, Exercises 2A and 2B – Track 7

A Hey, Danny, I am so tired this morning. I need a break. Let's get a cup of coffee.

B You're always tired on Mondays, Fernando. So, how was your weekend? Wild, as usual?

A Yeah, I guess. You know I like dancing, right? Well, last night, my girlfriend and I went to that new Cuban dance club – Club Havana.

B Oh, the one on, uh, Fourteenth Street?

A Yeah. Fourteenth Street. The place was full of people, and the music was incredible. We danced until, oh, it was about 1:30 in the morning. . . . Hey, you know what? You should come with us next time.

B Me? No. Oh, no. I don't like dancing.

A You're kidding. You don't like dancing? You really don't like dancing?

B Yeah, well, you know, Fernando, you're really outgoing and friendly, but I'm not outgoing. I'm not a party animal like you. I'm kind of shy. When I was a kid, I disliked going to parties, and I never learned how to dance.

A Really? That's too bad. But then, what do you enjoy doing?

B OK. This weekend, for example, I had a really nice, quiet weekend.

I worked on my car, I watched some TV, I studied for my business class, and . . .

A Wow, Danny! You mean you were home the whole time? You didn't go anywhere?

B Nope. I was home alone the whole weekend. Well, I went to the auto-parts store. See, I like staying home more than going out. But I'd like to find a girlfriend who likes staying home, too.

A A girlfriend? How are you going to find a girlfriend if you stay home all the time?

B Good question. Come on. Let's get back to work.

Page 7, Exercise 3A – Track 8

Fernando and Danny are talking about their weekend. Fernando is a very friendly and outgoing person. He enjoys dancing. Last night, he went to a dance club and stayed until late. Danny thinks Fernando is a party animal.

Danny is different from Fernando. He is shy and quiet. He dislikes dancing. Danny was home alone the whole weekend. He likes staying at home more than going out. He wants a girlfriend who likes staying home, too.

Page 12, Exercise 2 – Track 9

Your Personality and Your Job

What is the perfect job for you? It depends a lot on your personality. People think, act, and feel in different ways, and there are interesting jobs for every kind of person. Three common personality types are outgoing, intellectual, and creative.

Outgoing people enjoy meeting others and helping them. They are good talkers. They are friendly, and they get along well with other people. They often become nurses, counselors, teachers, or social workers.

Intellectual people like thinking about problems and finding answers to hard questions. They often enjoy reading and playing games like chess. Many intellectual people like working alone more than working in a group. They may become scientists, computer programmers, or writers.

Creative people enjoy making things. They like to imagine things that are new and different. Many of them become artists such as painters, dancers, or musicians. Architects, designers, and photographers are other examples of creative jobs.

Before you choose a career, think about your personality type. If you want to be happy in your work, choose the right job for your personality.

Unit 2: At school

Page 19, Exercises 2A and 2B – Track 10

A Hi, Alex.
B Hi, Bella.
A How long have you been in the library?
B For about two hours.
A How's it going?
B Um, not great.
A Why? What's the matter?
B I'm so discouraged. Look at this mess! I have to finish reading this book. Then I have to write a paper and study for a test. Where do I start!
A Well, Alex, have you ever tried making a to-do list?
B A to-do list?
A Yeah. You make a list of all the things you have to do. Then you do the most important things first.
B A to-do list. No, I've never tried that. I usually try to do six things at the same time. Let's see. Right now, the most important thing is to finish reading this book. But it's so boring. I can't concentrate.
A You need to be more active, Alex. Don't just read the book. You know, underline important ideas, write notes, repeat the main ideas to yourself. Those things will help you concentrate.
B Hmm. I think I can do that. But there's another problem.
A What's that?
B Too many new words! I can't remember all of them.
A Hmm. Well, here's an idea. Write important words on index cards. Take the cards with you, and study them everywhere – on the bus, during your break at work, and before you go to bed . . .
B OK, OK! I get it: study smarter – not harder. Thanks, Bella.

Page 19, Exercise 3A – Track 11

Alex has been at the library for a long time, and he is discouraged. He has many things to do. He needs to study for a test and write a paper. He needs to finish reading a book, but he can't concentrate. He says the book is boring.

Alex's friend Bella gives him some study advice. First, she tells Alex to make a list of all the things he needs to do. Next, she says he has to be a more active reader. Finally, she tells him to write vocabulary words on index cards and study them when he has free time. With Bella's help, Alex plans to study smarter, not harder.

Page 24, Exercise 2 – Track 12

Strategies for Learning English

Have you ever felt discouraged because it's hard to speak and understand English? Don't give up! Here are three strategies to help you learn faster and remember more.

Strategy # 1 – Set goals.

Have you ever set goals for learning English? When you set goals, you decide what you want to learn. After you determine your purpose for learning, you can make a plan to help you reach your goals. Maybe your goal is to learn more vocabulary. There are many ways to do this. For example, you can read in English for 15 minutes every day. You can also learn one new word every day.

Strategy # 2 – Look for opportunities to practice English.

Talk to everyone. Speak with people in the store, at work, and in the park. Don't worry about making mistakes. And don't forget to ask questions. For example, if your teacher uses a word you don't understand, ask a question like "What does that word mean?"

Strategy # 3 – Guess.

Don't try to translate every word. When you read, concentrate on clues such as pictures or other words in the sentence to help you understand. You can also make guesses when you are talking to people. For example, look at their faces and hand gestures – the way they move their hands – to help you guess the meaning.

Set goals, look for opportunities to practice, and guess. Do these things every day, and you will learn more English!

Unit 3: Friends and family

Page 33, Exercises 2A and 2B – Track 13

A Hello?
B Maria? Hi, It's Ana.
A Hey. Hi, Ana. How are you?
B Good, thanks. But I've been super busy. . . . Listen, Maria, do you have a minute to talk? Are you eating dinner?
A No, we've eaten. What's up?
B Well, I need a favor.
A Sure, Ana, what is it?
B The smoke alarm in my kitchen is beeping. *Beep, beep, beep.* I need to change the battery, but the ceiling's too high. Can I borrow your ladder?
A Sure, but I have a better idea. Um, Daniel can come over and change the battery for you.
B Really? Are you sure he has enough time?
A Oh, Ana, you know Daniel. He is never too busy to help a neighbor. He'll come over in five minutes.
B Thanks. I really appreciate it. I owe you one. See you . . .
A Wait, Ana, I want to ask you something. Did you hear our noisy neighbors last Saturday night? They had a party until three in the morning. Because of the noise, we couldn't sleep at all.

B Gosh, that's too bad, Maria. I didn't hear anything. But you should complain to the manager.
A Yeah, I know. I'll do it tomorrow.

Page 33, Exercise 3A – Track 14

Ana and Maria are neighbors. Ana calls Maria because she needs a favor. The smoke alarm in Ana's kitchen is beeping. She needs to change the battery, but the ceiling in her kitchen is too high. Ana asks to borrow Maria's ladder.

Maria says her husband, Daniel, will come over with a ladder and help Ana. Ana says, "I owe you one." This means she appreciates Maria and Daniel's help, and she will do a favor for them in the future.

Next, Maria tells Ana about their noisy neighbors. The neighbors had a party on Saturday night. Because of the noise, Maria and Daniel couldn't sleep. Ana tells Maria that she should complain to the apartment manager.

Page 38, Exercise 2 – Track 15

Neighborhood Watch Success Story
by Latisha Holmes, President, Rolling Hills Neighborhood Watch

People often ask me about the role of Neighborhood Watch. My answer is *Because of Neighborhood Watch, our neighborhood is safer and nicer.* Members of Neighborhood Watch help each other and look after the neighborhood. For example, we look after our neighbors' houses when they aren't home. We help elderly neighbors with yard work. Once a month, we get together to paint over graffiti.

Last Wednesday, the Neighborhood Watch team had another success story. Around 8:30 p.m., members of our Neighborhood Watch were out on a walk. Near the Corner Café, they noticed two men next to George Garcia's car. George lives on Rolling Hills Drive. The men were trying to break into the car. Suddenly, the car alarm went off. The men ran away and got into a car down the street. But they weren't quick enough. Our Neighborhood Watch members wrote down the car's license plate number and called the police. Later that night, the police arrested the two men.

I would like to congratulate our Neighborhood Watch team on their good work. Because so many people participate in Neighborhood Watch, Rolling Hills is a safer neighborhood today.

For information about Neighborhood Watch, please call 773-555-1234.

Unit 4: Health

Page 45, Exercises 2A and 2B – Track 16

A Hello, Stanley. I haven't seen you for some time. How've you been?

B Busy. I've been working really hard.

A I see. So what brings you here today?

B Well, you know, I've always been healthy, but, uh, I've been really tired lately.

A Uh-huh. Well, let's take a look at your chart. . . . Ah, I see you've gained 20 pounds since last year.

B Yeah. I used to exercise a lot, but now I just work. Work, eat, and sleep.

A Well, you know, gaining weight can make you feel tired, Stanley. You need to start exercising again. Can you try walking for 30 minutes each day?

B I don't have time. I'm working a lot these days – sometimes 10, even 12, hours a day.

A Hmm. Well, then, can you walk or ride a bicycle to work? And at work, don't use the elevator. Take the stairs.

B Well, I guess, I can try.

A Good. Now, let's see. You also have high blood pressure. Tell me about your diet. What have you eaten since yesterday?

B Well, last night I had a hamburger with fries and a soft drink.

A Fat, salt, and sugar! They're all bad for your blood pressure, Stanley. What about today?

B I haven't eaten anything today.

A No breakfast? Well, of course you feel tired! You need to change your diet, Stanley. Eat more fish and more vegetables. Give up fast food. No hamburgers! No fries! They're really bad for your health.

B That's really hard. I'm so busy right now. I don't have time to –

A Listen, Stanley. You're 40 years old. Do you want to have a heart attack? This is my advice. You need to make real changes, or you'll need to start taking pills and all kinds of medication.

B OK. I'll try.

Page 45, Exercise 3A – Track 17

Stanley is at the doctor's office. His health has always been good, but he has been really tired lately. The doctor looks at Stanley's chart. He sees a couple of problems. One problem is Stanley's weight. He has gained 20 pounds. Another problem is his blood pressure. The doctor tells him he needs regular exercise – for example, walking or riding a bike. He also tells Stanley to change his diet – to eat more fish and vegetables. If Stanley doesn't do these things, he will need to take pills and other medication. Stanley wants to be healthy, so he is going to try to follow the doctor's advice.

Page 50, Exercise 2 – Track 18

Two Beneficial Plants

Since the beginning of history, people in every culture have used plants to stay healthy and to prevent sickness. Garlic and chamomile are two beneficial plants.

Garlic is a plant in the onion family. The green stem and the leaves of the garlic plant grow above the ground. The root – the part under the ground – is a bulb with sections called cloves. They look like the pieces of an orange. The bulb is the part that people have traditionally used for medicine. They have used it for insect bites, cuts, earaches, and coughs. Today, some people also use it to treat high blood pressure and high cholesterol.

Chamomile is a small, pretty plant with flowers that bloom from late summer to early fall. The flowers have white petals and a yellow center. Many people use dried chamomile flowers to make tea. Some people give the tea to babies with upset stomachs. They also drink chamomile tea to feel better when they have a cold or the flu, poor digestion, or trouble falling asleep.

For thousands of years, people everywhere have grown garlic, chamomile, and other herbal medicines in their gardens. Today, you can buy them in health-food stores. You can get them in dried, powdered, or pill form.

Unit 5: Around town

Page 59, Exercises 2A and 2B – Track 19

A Mei, I'm so glad tomorrow is Friday. It's been a long week.

B That's for sure. Hmm. What would you like to do this weekend, Wen?

A Well, there are a few movies we haven't seen yet, or we could go to a concert downtown.

B Oh, we can't afford to go to concerts, Wen. They're too expensive. And I'm sort of tired of going to the movies.

A OK, so let's do something different on Sunday, something we haven't done yet this summer.

B Like what? Got any ideas?

A Let's check the newspaper for community events. Maybe we'll find something free right here in the neighborhood. Let's take a look. . . . Hmm. We have a lot of options. Here's something interesting. There's a concert in the park on Sunday at noon, admission is free.

B And here, look, there's a free walking tour of the gardens on Sunday at eleven o'clock.

A Here's another option, Mei. The Museum of Art is free the first Sunday of every month. There's an exhibit of modern art showing now. The museum opens at 10:00 a.m.

B Oh. And here's something at the library: free storytelling for children on Sunday at 10:30. Everything is happening on the same day at the same time! What do you want to do, Wen?

A Why don't we go to the library first?

B OK.

A Then, let's plan to go to the concert if the weather is nice. And then maybe later, we can go to the art museum.

B Yeah. That sounds good. I'll check the weather forecast for the weekend. Then we can decide.

Page 59, Exercise 3A – Track 20

It is Thursday. Wen and Mei are talking about their plans for the weekend. They can't afford to spend a lot of money on entertainment. They decide to check the newspaper for free community events on Sunday. They have many options. There's an outdoor concert in the park, a walking tour of the gardens, a modern art exhibit at the art museum, and storytelling for children at the library. All these events have free admission.

The problem is that all these things are happening on Sunday at the same time. Mei and Wen decide to take their son to the storytelling first. Then, if the weather is nice, they will go to the concert. Later, they might go to the art museum.

Page 64, Exercise 2 – Track 21

Salsa Starz at Century Park

If you missed the outdoor concert at Century Park last Saturday evening, you missed a great night of salsa music and dancing – and the admission was free!

The performers were the popular band Salsa Starz. Bandleader Ernesto Sanchez led the five-piece group and two dancers. Sanchez is a versatile musician. He sang and played maracas and guitar. The other musicians were also superb. The group's excellent playing and great energy galvanized the crowd. No one sat down during the entire show!

However, the evening had some problems. At first, the sound level of the music was excessive. I had to wear earplugs. Then, the level was too low. The change in sound was irritating. In addition, the stage was plain and unremarkable. I expected to see lights and lots of color at the performance. The weather was another problem. The night started out clear. By 10:00 p.m., some ominous black clouds moved in, and soon it started to rain. The band intended to play until eleven, but the show ended early because of the rain.

Century Park has free concerts every Saturday evening in July and August. If you haven't attended one of these concerts yet, plan to go next weekend. But take an umbrella!

Unit 6: Time

Page 71, Exercises 2A and 2B – Track 22

A Winston, what are you doing?
B I'm thinking.
A No, you're not. You're procrastinating. You always procrastinate. I'm getting very impatient with you! I asked you to take out the trash two hours ago, and you haven't done it yet.
B Aw, Mom.
A Do you have homework?
B Yeah, but . . . I can't decide what to do first.
A Hmm. Would you like some help?
B Well, uh, yeah, I guess.
A OK. So, why don't you make a to-do list. You know, write down all the tasks you have to do.
B OK. I've got . . . math, an English essay, and a history project.
A Uh-huh. What else?
B I have to practice guitar. I have a lesson tomorrow.
A And don't forget the trash. Write that down, too.
B OK. Now what?
A Prioritize. What are you going to do first, second, third, and so on?
B Well, guitar is first. It's the most fun.
A Nuh-uh. I don't think so. Homework and chores are first. Guitar is last.
B OK. Should I start with math, English, or history?
A Hmm. When are they due?
B Math and English are due tomorrow.
A And the history project?
B The deadline is next week. On Tuesday.
A OK. So do math and English tonight. You can do the history project over the weekend.
B OK, math and English tonight. Which one should I do first?
A Well, I always do the hardest thing first.
B English is a lot harder than math.
A OK. So English, then math, then guitar. But before you do anything . . .
B Yeah, I know. Take out the trash.
A Right.

Page 71, Exercise 3A – Track 23

Winston is listening to music in his room. His mother comes in and tells him to stop procrastinating. She is very impatient because he isn't taking out the trash and he isn't doing his homework.

Winston has too many things to do. His mother suggests making a to-do list. First, she tells him to list all the tasks he needs to do. Next, she tells him to prioritize – to put his tasks in order of importance. His mother says he needs to do his homework and chores first. He decides to do his English and math homework first because they are due the next day. He also has a history project, but the deadline is next Tuesday. After he finishes his homework, he will practice guitar. But before he does anything else, he has to take out the trash.

Page 76, Exercise 2 – Track 24
Rules About Time

Every culture has rules about time. These rules are usually unspoken, but everybody knows them.

In some countries such as the United States, England, and Canada, punctuality is an unspoken rule. It is important to be on time, especially in business. People usually arrive a little early for business appointments. Business meetings and personal appointments often have strict beginning and ending times. When you are late, other people might think you are rude, disorganized, or irresponsible.

These countries also have cultural rules about time in social situations. For example, when an invitation for dinner says 6:00 p.m., it is impolite to arrive more than five or ten minutes late. On the other hand, when the invitation is for a party from 6:00 to 8:00 or a reception from 3:30 to 5:30, you can arrive anytime between those hours. For public events with specific starting times – movies, concerts, sports events – you should arrive a few minutes before the event begins. In fact, some theaters do not allow people to enter if they arrive after the event has started.

Other cultures have different rules about time. In Brazil, it is not unusual for guests to arrive an hour or two after a social event begins. In the Philippines, it is not uncommon for people to miss scheduled events – a class or an appointment – to meet a friend at the airport. Many Filipinos believe that relationships with people are more important than keeping a schedule.

Unit 7: Shopping

Page 85, Exercises 2A and 2B – Track 25

A Julie, look at this car! "Automatic transmission, air-conditioning, leather seats, sun roof, power windows . . ." It's got everything, and it's only $27,500.
B Ken, are you crazy? With tax and fees, that's about $30,000! We can't afford $30,000 for a car! Where . . . where are we going to get the money? The balance in our savings account is less than $8,000!
A No problem. Look here. It says, "Special financing available. Only 4 percent interest with 60 months to pay off the loan!"
B Sixty months to pay! That's five years! We're going to pay for that car every month for five years. Ken, you know I'm afraid of getting into debt. We have bills to pay every month, and we need to save money for college for the kids.
A Well, Julie, tell me: Do we need a car, or don't we need a car? Our old one always needs repair, and it's . . .
B OK, OK. We do need a car. But we don't need a new car. We could look for a used car. Let's go across the street and look. I'm sure we can find a good used car for $10,000 or even less than that.
A Yeah, but, Julie, look at this car. It's a beauty! We should get it. We can buy the car on credit. Everybody does it!
B No, not everybody! My father always paid cash for everything. He didn't even have a credit card!
A Well, your father never had any fun. And, I'm not your father!

Page 85, Exercise 3A – Track 26

Ken and his wife, Julie, are looking at cars. Ken wants to buy a new car that costs over $27,000. Julie thinks that they can't afford to spend that much money. The balance in their savings account is less than $8,000. She's afraid of getting into debt. But Ken says they can get financing to help pay for the new car. The interest rate is low, and they can take five years to pay off the loan. Ken isn't worried about buying things on credit.

Julie disagrees. She suggests that they could buy a used car. She says her father never had a credit card. He always paid cash for everything.

Page 90, Exercise 2 – Track 27
A Credit Card Nightmare

Sun Hi and Joseph Kim got their first credit card a week after they got married. At first, they paid off the balance every month.

The couple's problems began after they bought a new house. They bought new furniture, a big-screen television, and two new computers. To pay for everything, they applied for more and more credit. Soon they had six different credit cards, and they were more than $18,000 in debt.

"It was a nightmare!" says Mrs. Kim. "The interest rates were 19 percent to 24 percent. Our minimum payments were over $750 a month. We both got second jobs, but it wasn't enough. I was so worried about paying off the debt, I cried all the time."

Luckily, the Kims found a solution. They met Dolores Delgado, a debt counselor. With her help, they looked at all of their living expenses and made a family budget. They combined their six credit card payments into one monthly payment with a lower interest rate. Now, their monthly budget for all living expenses is $3,400. Together they earn $3,900 a month. That leaves $500 for paying off their debt.

"We've cut up our credit cards," says Mr. Kim. "No more expensive furniture! In five years, we can pay off our debt. Now we know. Credit cards are dangerous!

Unit 8: Work

Page 97, Exercises 2A and 2B – Track 28

A Good morning, Tony. Thanks for coming in. I'm Ken Leong, personnel manager for the company.

B Nice to meet you, Mr. Leong.

A So, I have your résumé right here, and I understand you're interested in the job of shipping-and-receiving clerk.

B Yes, that's right. I'm applying for the shipping-and-receiving clerk position.

A OK. I'd like to ask you a few questions.

B Sure, go ahead.

A Uh. First of all, could you tell me a little about your background? Where are you from? What kind of work have you done?

B Well, I was born in Peru and lived there for 18 years. I finished high school there, and then I came here with my family. I've been living here for two years.

A OK. And are you currently employed?

B Uh. Sorry?

A Are you working now?

B Yes, I've been working part-time as a teacher's assistant at an elementary school for about a year. And I'm also going to community college at night. I want to get a degree in accounting.

A Oh. That's good. What office machines can you use?

B Uh. I can use a computer, a fax machine, a scanner, and a copying machine.

A Excellent. Those skills will be useful in this job. You'll need to take inventory and order supplies. Now, Tony, can you tell me about some of your strengths?

B Um. Excuse me?

A Your strengths – you know, your personal qualities. What makes you a good person for this job?

B Well, I'm very responsible and reliable. If I have a deadline, I come in early or stay late to finish the job. Also, I get along with everyone. I never have problems working with people. I like everyone, and they like me.

A That's great. Can you work any shift?

B Well, I prefer the day shift because I have classes at night.

A OK, Tony. There's going to be an opening in the day shift soon. I'll get back to you next week sometime.

B Thank you, Mr. Leong. I appreciate that. It was nice to meet you.

A You, too. I'll give you a call.

Page 97, Exercise 3A – Track 29

Tony has been working as a teacher's assistant for about a year. He is also going to college part-time to get a degree in accounting. Right now, Tony is at a job interview with Mr. Leong, the personnel manager.

Mr. Leong asks about Tony's background. Tony says he is from Peru and has been living in the United States for two years. Next, Mr. Leong asks about Tony's work experience, and Tony says that now he is employed at a school. Finally, Mr. Leong asks about Tony's personal strengths. Tony says he is responsible and reliable, and he gets along with everybody. Mr. Leong says he will contact Tony next week.

Page 102, Exercise 2 – Track 30

Eden's Blog

Monday 9/29

I had my interview today! I gave the interviewer a big smile and a firm handshake. I answered her questions with confidence. I'll let you know if I get the job.

Thursday 9/25

Great news! One of the companies from the job fair finally called me back! I've been preparing for the job interview all day. I'm really excited. I'm going to have a practice interview with some classmates today. That will prepare me for the real one.

Wednesday 9/24

I've been feeling depressed about the job search lately, but my counselor at school told me I shouldn't give up. He said I need to be patient. Today, I organized my papers. I made lists of the places I have applied to and the people I have talked to. I also did some more research online.

Tuesday 9/16

Today, I went to a job fair at my college. I filled out several applications and handed out some résumés. There were about 20 different companies there. Several of them said they were going to call me back. Wish me luck!

Monday 9/15

Hello fellow job searchers! I have been looking for a job for several weeks. Everyone tells me that it's critical to network, so I've been telling everyone I know. I've been calling friends, relatives, and teachers to tell them about my job search. If you have any good job-searching tips, please share them with me!

Unit 9: Daily living

Page 111, Exercises 2A and 2B – Track 31

A Hello?

B Samantha, this is Monica.

A Monica! I've been waiting for you to call. But, um, you sound really strange. Are you OK?

B Well, actually, no! I'm not. . . . Not at all. Somebody broke into our house tonight.

A Broke into your house? That's terrible! When? How?

B Well, around 7:30, we went over to the Morenos' next door to watch a movie. And while we were there, someone broke into our house and robbed us. They stole our TV, DVD player, jewelry, and some cash. I still can't believe it.

A Ugh. That's awful. How did the robber get in?

B He broke a window in the back bedroom. You should see the mess – there's glass all over the floor, and there are books and CDs and clothes all over the place. And, Samantha, they took my mother's ring. I'm so upset.

A Oh, did you call the police?

B Of course. They've already been here.

A What's happening to our neighborhood? We never used to have so much crime. When the kids were little, we didn't even lock the front door!

B Well, I'm just glad we weren't home when it happened.

A Oh, Monica, I feel so bad for you. And I'm worried. Did you hear someone robbed Mr. Purdy last week, too, while he was out taking a walk? I think we should start a Neighborhood Watch program, don't you?

B Yeah, we've been talking about that for months. I agree, it's time we finally did it. But right now, I have to clean up this mess.

A Do you want me to come over, Monica? I could help you clean up.

B You're the best, Samantha. Yeah, come as quickly as you can. Thanks.

Page 111, Exercise 3A – Track 32

Monica calls Samantha with bad news. While Monica and Todd were out, someone broke into their home and stole their TV, DVD player, jewelry, and some cash. Monica is upset because the robber took her mother's ring. She says the person got in through a window in the back bedroom.

Samantha is worried. She says they never used to have so much crime in their neighborhood. She tells Monica that last week someone robbed their neighbor Mr. Purdy, too. Samantha thinks they should start a Neighborhood Watch program. Monica agrees, but first she needs to clean up the mess in her house. Samantha offers to come over and help.

Page 116, Exercise 2 – Track 33

Home Is More Than a Building

A few months ago, Pedro Ramirez, 45, lost his job in a grocery store. To pay the bills, he got a part-time job at night. Several days later, Pedro's wife, Luisa, gave him a big surprise. She was pregnant with their sixth child. Pedro was happy but worried. "How am I going to support another child without a full-time job?" he wondered.

That evening, Pedro and Luisa got some more news. A fire was coming near their home. By the next morning, the fire was very close. The police ordered every family in the neighborhood to evacuate. The Ramirez family moved quickly. While Pedro was gathering their legal documents, Luisa grabbed the family photographs, and the children put their pets – a cat and a bird – in the family's van. Then, the family drove to the home of Luisa's sister, one hour away.

About 24 hours later, Pedro and Luisa got very bad news. The fire destroyed their home. They lost almost everything. With no home, only part-time work, and a baby coming, Pedro was even more worried about the future.

For the next three months, the Ramirez family stayed with Luisa's sister while workers were rebuilding their home. Many generous people helped them during that difficult time. Friends took them shopping for clothes. Strangers left gifts at their door. A group of children collected $500 to buy bicycles for the Ramirez children.

Because of all the help from friends and neighbors, the Ramirez family was able to rebuild their lives. Two months after the fire, Luisa mailed out holiday cards with this message: "Home is more than a building. Home is wherever there is love."

Unit 10: Free time

Page 123, Exercises 2A and 2B – Track 34

A I'm so exhausted! I really need a vacation.

B You know, my work is pretty slow right now. I can talk to my boss. Maybe he'll give me a few days off.

A Oh, Ricardo, what a great idea. We haven't had a family vacation in two years.

B Where would you like to go, Felicia?

A We could go to San Francisco. Michelle's six – she's old enough to enjoy it, don't you think?

B Well, let's see if there are any deals on any of the Internet travel sites. . . . Look, if we book a flight seven days ahead, we can get a round-trip ticket for $200.

A That's not too expensive. Are there any discounts for children?

B Hmm. Let's see . . . I don't think so.

A Oh, that's too bad. What about hotel rates?

B Not cheap. Summer is the height of the tourist season. If we stay in a nice hotel, it's going to cost at least $250 a night.

A Plus the room tax, don't forget. You have to add on an extra 14 percent or something like that.

B Right. I forgot about that. So if the three of us take this trip, and if we stay in San Francisco just three days, it's going to cost almost $1,200.

A That's a lot to spend for just a three-day vacation, Ricardo. Maybe we should just go camping instead.

B Yeah, you're probably right. We could go to Big Bear Lake. If we do that, how much will it cost?

A Well, gas will probably cost about $100, the campsite will cost about $35 a night, and then there's food – but that won't be too much if we grill hamburgers.

B Michelle will probably have more fun camping, too.

A I agree. So what do you think? Should we make a reservation?

B I'll reserve the campsite after I talk to my boss tomorrow.

A I hope he says yes. We really need a vacation.

Page 123, Exercise 3A – Track 35

Felicia is exhausted. She needs a vacation. Her husband, Ricardo, says he can ask his boss for a few days off. Felicia would like to go to San Francisco. They look for special travel discounts on the Internet. If they book a flight at least seven days ahead, they can get a round-trip ticket for less than $200. On the other hand, hotel room rates will be high because summer is the most popular tourist season. Also, there is a room tax on hotel rooms in San Francisco. They figure out that a three-day trip to San Francisco will cost almost $1,200.

Felicia and her husband decide to change their plans. If they go camping, they will save a lot of money and their daughter will have more fun. Felicia's husband will reserve the campsite after he talks to his boss.

Page 128, Exercise 2 – Track 36

The Rock: San Francisco's Biggest Tourist Attraction

Alcatraz, a small, rocky island in the middle of San Francisco Bay, was once the most famous prison in the United States. For a period of 29 years, from 1934 to 1963, over 1,500 dangerous criminals lived in the prison's 378 cells. People believed that it was impossible to escape from Alcatraz Island. However, in 1962, two brothers, John and Clarence Anglin, and another man named Frank Morris escaped on a raft made of raincoats. A famous movie, Escape from Alcatraz, tells this amazing story. Other famous prisoners who lived on the island included Al Capone, the gangster, and Robert Stroud, the "Birdman of Alcatraz."

Alcatraz prison closed in 1963. The island became a national park, and since then, it has been a major attraction for tourists from all over the world. These days, many people call Alcatraz by its popular name, "The Rock."

In the summer, it is wise to buy tickets to the island in advance because the ferries sell out. Evening tours are less crowded. The admission prices listed include the ferry, tickets, and an audio tour.

General admission:
Adult (18–61), $36.00
Junior (12–17), $34.50
Child (5–11), $26.00
Senior (62 or older), $34.50

Illustration credits

Kenneth Batelman: 87, 101

Cyrille Berger: 35, 100, 125

Nina Edwards: 34, 127

Travis Foster: 9, 36, 47, 114

Chuck Gonzales: 10, 75, 89, 115

Brad Hamann: 37, 38, 49, 73, 118

Q2A Media Services: 2, 9 (#6), 17, 43, 55, 69, 81, 92, 107, 113

Monika Roe: 93, 116

Photography credits

Track (STUDENT TK) Listing for Self-Study Audio CD

Track	Page	Exercise	Track	Page	Exercise	Track	Page	Exercise
1			13	33	2A and 2B	25	85	2A and 2B
2	3	2A	14	33	3A	26	85	3A
3	4	3A	15	38	2	27	90	2
4	4	3B	16	45	2A and 2B	28	97	2A and 2B
5	5	4A and 4B	17	45	3A	29	97	3A
6	5	4C	18	50	2	30	102	2
7	7	2A and 2B	19	59	2A and 2B	31	111	2A and 2B
8	7	3A	20	59	3A	32	111	3A
9	12	2	21	64	2	33	116	2
10	19	2A and 2B	22	71	2A and 2B	34	123	2A and 2B
11	19	3A	23	71	3A	35	123	3A
12	24	2	24	76	2	36	128	2